PS
desserts

To my sisters Nin and Jose,
for making all the right noises.

Published in 2011 by Hardie Grant Books

Hardie Grant Books (Australia)
Ground Floor, Building 1
658 Church Street
Richmond, Victoria 3181
www.hardiegrant.com.au

Hardie Grant Books (UK)
Second Floor, North Suite
Dudley House, Southampton Street
London WC2E 7HF
www.hardiegrant.co.uk

Publisher: Paul McNally
Project editor: Gordana Trifunovic
Design manager: Heather Menzies
Designer: Gayna Murphy
Editor: Belinda So
Photographer: Mark Roper
Stylist: Leesa O'Reilly
Paper artist: Benja Harney

The publisher would like to thank the following
for their generosity in supplying props for the book:
Hub Furniture, The Essential Ingredient, Market Import,
Simon Johnson and KitchenAid.

National Library of Australia Cataloguing-in-Publication Data:
Sibley, Philippa. PS desserts / Philippa Sibley.
ISBN 978 1 74270 204 9 (hbk.) Desserts.
641.86

Printed and bound in China by 1010 Printing International Limited.
Colour reproduction by Splitting Image Colour Studio
Copyright text © Philippa Sibley 2011
Copyright photography © Hardie Grant Books 2011

Ps
desserts

Philippa Sibley

Foreword By Christine Manfield

hardie grant books

MELBOURNE · LONDON

Contents

Basics

Recipes

Foreword

I have known Philippa as a friend and a colleague since she first arrived back in Australia in the mid-nineties. We cooked together at Mietta's, then at est est est and Ondine, where her reputation was cemented for her seminal dessert work. Ever since, we have connected regularly over our shared love of sugar and flavour.

Philippa brings a fresh energy, a mature wisdom and a thoroughly knowledgeable intelligence to her desserts and the pastry kitchen. Her passion is palpable as you read through the pages of her book. She is sharing so many of her secrets and generously provides tips and suggestions, holding your hand along the way as you discover her beautiful desserts.

Her skillful attention to detail in each recipe with step-by-step guides provides an important training tool, a must for keen cooks everywhere.

The images are visually stunning and this book encapsulates Philippa's philosophy on the flavours and textures of desserts with a strong emphasis on technique and artful presentation. I hope you find this book as inspiring as I do, that you take it to your heart like I have, that you embrace the dessert world the way Philippa has and expand your knowledge and repertoire of all the possibilities in the sugar world.

You will find plenty to fall in love with.

Christine Manfield
Universal Restaurant 2011

Introduction

When I started thinking about writing this book, my main aim was to demystify desserts. There seems to be so much secrecy behind creating perfect puff pastry, an impressive crème brûlée or super-smooth sorbet. I thought it was time to share the techniques I've honed over my years in the kitchen.

I started out my career as a chef and became a pastry chef early on but it was in London, and then in France, that my passion for pastry really came out. It was there that I learnt so many of the techniques that I've shared in my book. I returned to Australia and became well-known for my pastry skills.

My love of creating desserts came when I discovered the joy of freshly churned ice cream, tarts served within only hours of being baked, and couveture chocolate… What a difference! Once I had mastered the classics, it became easier to play with ingredients and experiment with different techniques — which is why this is the foundation of this book . Before you even begin cooking, you first need to know the basics — all those techniques that come together to create a sensational dessert. I'm sharing with you the knowledge I have gained over so many years — knowledge that is often kept as a closely guarded secret by most chefs!

I want everyone to realise that they can make these desserts at home. You don't need tricky equipment, a commercial kitchen, or impossible-to-find ingredients. You just need patience and a willingness to try — and then try again. You might fail at your first attempt but you'll soon learn where you went wrong and do better next time. If you love desserts, then these skills are worth spending the time to master.

I don't think desserts should be taken too seriously. They should be playful, and enjoyed whenever you feel like it. I've given you the framework but that doesn't mean you can't enjoy the process. The desserts taste better when you've had a great time creating them. I don't have a huge sweet tooth. For me, creating desserts has facilitated my own kind of a spectator sport. People enjoying what I have made, makes it beyond worthwhile. I hope you'll get that same feeling when you create something deliciously sweet for the people around you.

This book should help convince both pastry cooks and home cooks that making great desserts is fun and accessible. Don't be afraid of the technical side of things — build your repetoire, practise, make a mess. And most of all: enjoy!

Special Notes

Listed over the next few pages are my "can't-do-without utensils". Most items are readily available at kitchenware stores but there are a few tools that you will need to pick up at specialty baking shops or online.

The following equipment is in no particular order and, it goes without saying, an electric mixer, food processor and ice-cream machine are my essential items.

Invest in the right equipment and you will be off to the best start. Modern-day gadgets and kitchen machinery are a luxury that I never take for granted. You don't need to buy every piece of equipment available though. Buy what you need as you go, so you don't end up with drawers full of things you will never use. Try to buy the best quality you can afford as equipment will last longer and it will be worth the investment, especially for items you'll be using often.

Equipment 1

1. SPRINGFORM CAKE TIN

2 & 14. SMALL AND LARGE LOAF TINS

3. DARIOLE MOULDS
These are the ideal portion size — 125 ml.
I prefer metal moulds rather than plastic
ones because, when you come to turning
things like a panna cotta out, typically by
dipping in hot water, they conduct heat
better, making the job much easier.

4. EXTRA-LARGE PASTRY CUTTER
I use this as a stencil to cut out pie lids
or tart bases.

5. COOLING RACK

6. BAKING TRAYS
Along with rectangular trays, I like to use
aluminium pizza trays. They're the perfect
shape and size for cakes and tarts and you
can use them for serving.

7. MUSLIN CLOTH
Ideal for super-fine sieving. It's essential
when straining liquids to capture fine
sediment, such as when extracting pure
fruit juices.

8. SMALL TART SHELLS
These are used to make petits fours.

9. BROWNIE TRAY

10. SMALL TART RINGS
These are great to use as moulds for tart
shells (rather than loose-bottomed tart
tins) because you can lift the rings straight
off without having to fiddle with the shell.

11 & 13. DESSERT RINGS
The charm of using these for moulding
desserts like my mousse, rice pudding and
chocolate biscuit is that it eliminates double
handling. You can prepare the dessert on
the serving plate, then with a quick flash
from a blowtorch to loosen the ring, you
can lift it off.

12. SILICONE BAKING MAT
A non-stick reusable mat for baking cakes,
macarons and biscuits.

Equipment 1

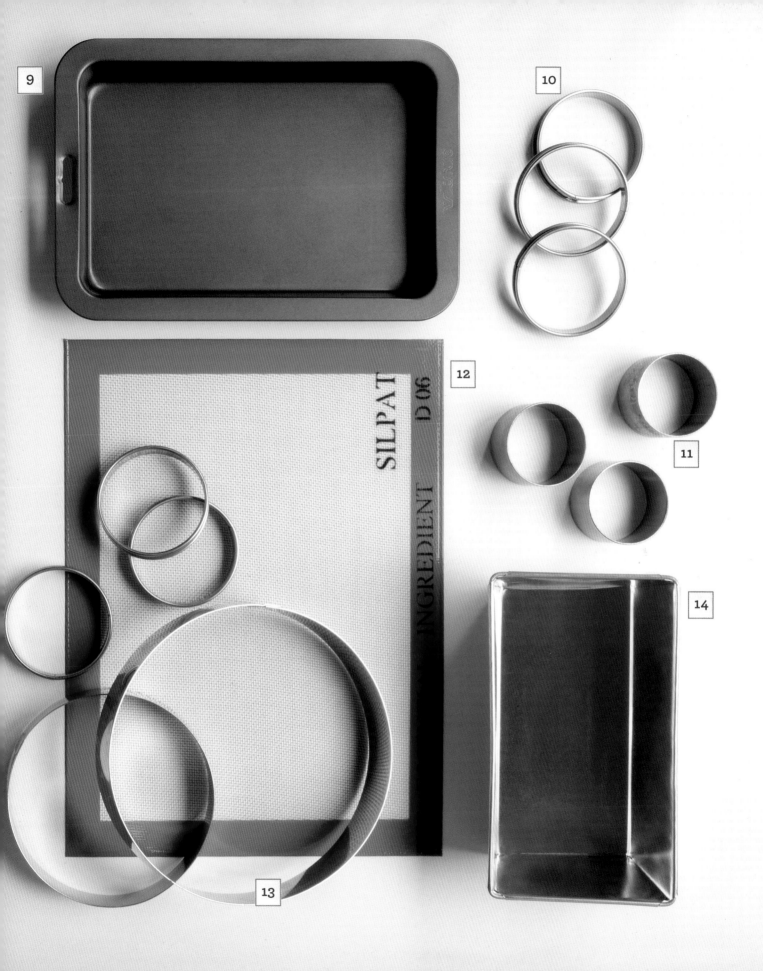

Equipment 2

1. **SIEVE**

2. **PASTRY CUTTERS**

3. **SCULPTURED RUBBER SPATULA**
The curved sides means you can get every last bit from a saucepan or bowl.

4. **PASTRY DOCKER**
Used for punching holes in raw pastry to prevent it from rising too much.

5. **MEASURING SPOONS**

6. **ROLLING PIN**

7. **BALLOON WHISK**

8. **STAINLESS-STEEL WHISKS**

9. **WOODEN SPOONS**
Always keep wooden spoons specifically for pastry and desserts separate from those used for savoury applications. They are very porous and once they have soaked up a smell, such as onion, the odour will permeate everything it comes into contact with.

10. **DIGITAL SUGAR THERMOMETER**
An indispensable tool that takes the guesswork out of measuring the temperature of liquids. Invest in a digital version, which is inexpensive and accurate.

11. **SLOTTED SPOON**

12. **ASSORTED MELON (PARISIAN) SCOOPS**

13. **PASTRY BRUSHES**
I have on hand various sizes and keep their uses separate for savoury and sweet applications. If you have dipped your brush in eggwash, always rinse the brush in cold water — not hot — before washing, otherwise the heat will cook the egg onto the bristles.

14. **CITRUS JUICER**

15. **SCRAPER**
A straight, hard scraper used for chocolate work to make garnishes like "cigarettes".

16. **HEATPROOF RUBBER SPATULA**
Buy a heatproof one so you can fold creams and work with other hot mixtures.

17. **FINE MICROPLANE**

18. **STEP-PALETTE KNIFE**
The step allows you to spread things like chocolate more evenly and flatter on a surface than a regular palette knife.

19. **ASSORTED PALETTE KNIVES**
Essential tools of the trade used for spreading, lifting and decoration.

20. **PEELER**

Equipment 2

Golden Rules

1. Use the finest ingredients you can afford or find.

2. Believe in the seasons. Use fruit at its best.

3. Have all your equipment ready before you begin.

4. Weigh all your ingredients before beginning the recipe and keep them separate.

5. Always preheat the oven as directed.

6. Prepare what you can in advance. This saves time and stress.

7. Read through the whole recipe before starting, so you know what is involved in each step.

8. Follow the directions carefully— taking shortcuts may result in having to start over.

9. Don't be disheartened if it doesn't turn out perfectly. Practise, practise, practise ...

10. Have fun!

Notes on Eggs

Without eggs the world of desserts would be a different place altogether. No soufflés, sponge cakes or luxurious ice-creams. Heaven forbid! I have learnt a few things over the years about eggs and how best to deal with these crucial little packages.

SIZE

As you will discover in the following recipes, I give the weight of eggwhites and egg yolks because eggs can differ in size considerably; if you're using 50 g eggs, the yolks and whites will be considerably smaller than those of a 70 g egg. As a general rule of thumb, an egg yolk typically weighs 20 g and a white is 30 g. The best way to ensure your quantities are correct is to weigh your yolks and whites every time. Weighing is especially helpful when you have whites left over from another recipe (from making a crème anglaise, for example).

EQUIPMENT

When whisking eggwhite, ensure that your utensils are very clean and dry. Anything oily, wet or in any way foreign may ruin the result you're after.

STORING

I store eggs in the fridge — I find they separate much more easily as the yolk and white stay firmer, and they remain fresher than if they were stored at room temperature.

Eggwhite freezes beautifully and, as a plus, the proteins slightly break down during the freezing process and whisk up better than fresh whites. It's useful to freeze eggwhite in batches of 50 g and 100 g. When you want to use them, thaw in the fridge overnight.

Egg yolks don't freeze as successfully as whites, but they do store quite well in the fridge, sprinkled with a little water and with plastic wrap pressed directly onto the surface. They will keep (depending on their initial freshness) for up to a week.

COOKING

Egg yolks set and pasteurise at just above 80°C, so if you're unsure, for example when making a crème anglaise, use a thermometer.

WHISKING EGGWHITE

Often in recipes for mousses or soufflés, people tend to over-whisk the eggwhite. To ensure a beautiful texture or rise, it is very important that the whites are whisked to hold "soft peaks" only (see page 102). Over-whisked whites will become grainy and watery (referred to as "snowy") because the proteins break down and separate.

When making a meringue (see page 100), sugar is added and, as a result, the eggwhite will be more stable and there is less chance of over-whisking the mixture.

Notes on Fruit

I love using fruit in my desserts, but only when it is in peak condition. In Melbourne, where I live, seasonality is a very important factor when it comes to quality. The seasons really do dictate the desserts I make. When the first cherries appear, I think of the nearness of summer and all the beautiful stone fruits that I associate with Christmas. Then come the late-summer berries and figs in autumn. In winter, the citrus fruits arrive in all their glory: honey murcott mandarins, blood oranges and ruby grapefruit, which are all at their best. Quinces, pears and apples feature strongly on my winter dessert menus too.

CHOOSING

Remember, fruit should be sweet and fragrant. When choosing fruit such as berries, always look at the bottom of the punnet to check the fruit (often under-ripe or squashed fruit is hidden under the nicer-looking fruit).Also use your sense of smell. If the strawberries smell and look beautiful, they probably are.

When choosing melons, feel for weight and firmness. Pineapples should have a golden hue and if you pull a leaf, it should pluck out easily. Pears are a tricky one; I always buy slightly under-ripe green pears and let them ripen for several days before poaching. If using peaches for poaching, they should be perfectly ripe or their skins will not slip off and the flavour won't be as luscious. When feeling a peach for ripeness, always press near the base as you don't want to bruise the fruit on its presentation side.

When choosing fruit for sorbets, I encourage you to stick with seasonal fruit in its best condition — average fruit makes average sorbet. An exception is frozen berries, such as raspberries and blackberries, which make very lovely sorbet (but not strawberries as they "cook" in the freezer and will taste jammy when defrosted).

STORING

Most fruits are best kept in the fridge, but only if they are ripe. Peaches, for example, will stop ripening in the fridge and their skin may become leathery and wrinkled but the flesh will stay hard. Don't keep delicate fruits, such as stone fruits or pears, in bags on top of each other or jumbled together as they will likely bruise or become damaged, and this will affect their final presentation. Fruit is a fragile ingredient.

If you have an excess of peaches, nectarines or apricots, these freeze well. Halve and remove the stones and, in the case of peaches or nectarines, blanch and remove the skins before freezing, laid out on a tray. Once frozen, place in freezer bags in 500 g batches, ready to use later.

Notes on Chocolate

The quality of chocolate available has improved
enormously. Gone are the days when "cooking"
chocolate was used for cakes and mousses.
Today couverture chocolate is readily found,
even at the humble corner store.

TYPES

Swiss, Spanish and French couverture chocolate are the most widely available and the range is huge — from single origin (beans sourced from only one particular area) to amazing blends of varying percentages from 50 per cent cocoa solids to 100 per cent. My favourite percentage is between 65 per cent and 75 per cent as anything higher can be quite bitter.

Milk chocolate is blended with sugar and milk powder and should have at least 30 per cent cocoa solids, but can have as much as 50 per cent or even higher. However, white chocolate contains no cocoa solids at all.

Due to the different amounts of fats, cocoa and sugar in dark, milk and white chocolate, they cannot be successfully interchanged in recipes. For example, if you use white chocolate to make my Brownies (see page 114), the result will be greasy and over-sweet. So white chocolate lovers take note!

Generally, the better the chocolate the more you pay, but you'll find the smooth, creamy, melt-in-your-mouth results are well worth it.

STORING

Always keep at room temperature, well wrapped.

WORKING WITH CHOCOLATE

Melting and tempering chocolate is one of the essentials of pastry technique (see pages 186–9). It's important not to allow the chocolate to get too hot as it burns at a very low temperature. If it does burn, it will "seize" and become unworkable. White chocolate is especially volatile.

Notes on Butter for Pastry

My colleagues, family and friends can attest to my obsession with butter. Butter is made from cream, right? Cream is white not daffodil yellow. Butter is a fresh food and should look and smell as such. It should have a faint, creamy, slightly sweet smell. If it is rancid, yellow and sour, I don't use it.

BUYING

Always check the use-by date on the pack and only use unsalted butter for pastry and baking.

USING

It's important your butter is at a workable temperature when making pastry. None of my pastry recipes uses cold butter straight from the fridge. "Room temperature" butter is a tricky definition as it depends on the room. This is why I've chosen to demonstrate with photos the ideal texture of butter for making pastry.

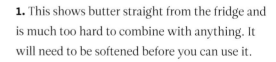

1. This shows butter straight from the fridge and is much too hard to combine with anything. It will need to be softened before you can use it.

2. This shows butter in the perfect state: malleable, not too hard or melting.

3. This shows butter that has softened too much. It is far too soft for pastry work and will result in an oily product.

Basics

Pâtes & Pastries

Pâte Sucrée
Pâte Sablée
Sablé Breton
Puff Pastry
Brioche

Pâte Sucrée

This sweet pastry is your dessert workhorse. Not only is it a delicious support act to many other ingredients, the pastry itself is not too "short", so it's easy to work with. Short refers to the texture of the pastry. The more butter it has, the shorter or more delicate and crumbly it becomes. I use this pastry in my Lemon Tart (see page 208) and Fruit Tartlets (see page 216). Make the full quantity because you can always freeze the portion you don't use.

Makes 1.1 kg (enough to line 2 large tart rings)

360 g butter, softened (see page 28)
150 g pure icing sugar, sifted
4 egg yolks
50 ml cold water
500 g plain flour, sifted
a pinch of cooking salt
1 egg yolk, lightly beaten,
   for brushing

EQUIPMENT
sieve
electric mixer
palette knife or scraper
rolling pin
tart ring/s
baking tray
uncooked rice (for baking)
pastry brush

MAKING THE DOUGH

1. Place the butter in the bowl of an electric mixer fitted with a paddle attachment. Work the butter on low speed until smooth and the same texture.

2. Add the icing sugar and mix together on medium speed until combined, taking care not to aerate too much — you don't want it pale and fluffy.

NOTE
- Pâte is the French term for a pastry dough or sometimes refers to a batter. (It's pronounced paht — not to be confused with pâté.)

3. In a separate bowl, combine the 4 egg yolks and water. While still mixing, add to the butter mixture bit by bit. At this stage the mixture may look as though it has separated, but once the flour is added, this will be rectified.

5

4. Now turn off the mixer, then tip in the flour and salt. On low speed, work in the flour and salt until the mixture comes together and is crumbly. Do not overwork at this stage as the gluten in the flour will activate and the pastry could become tough.

5. Tip the contents of the bowl onto a work surface and, using the heel of your hand, smear the mixture away from you until it looks smooth and no patches of butter remain.

6. Using a palette knife or scraper, scrape the pastry together into a mound. Divide the mound of pastry in half and pat each half into about 3 cm-high rounds — you don't want a big boulder otherwise it will make it harder later to achieve the right temperature to work the dough. Wrap in plastic wrap and refrigerate until chilled all the way through.

WORKING THE DOUGH

7. Once the dough has chilled, remove it from the fridge and place on a work surface lightly dusted with flour. Chop the dough into manageable bits and smear each bit with the heel of your hand to get the dough going. If you missed any bits of butter before, make sure you smear them out this time.

8. Once the pastry is all the same texture, bring it all together again.

9. Shape the pastry back into a ball, ready to roll out.

10. Gently but firmly tap the pastry out slightly with your rolling pin to get things going.

11. Roll the pastry quickly so it doesn't warm up too much and become soft and unmanageable. Roll evenly and make a one-quarter turn every couple of rolls to keep the shape.

NOTE
- This pastry freezes well. Freeze at the end of step 6. Remove from the freezer and thaw overnight in the fridge before rolling out.

LINING THE TART RING

12. Line a baking tray with baking paper and place a tart ring on top.

13. Roll the pastry out to a thickness of about 5 mm. The pastry should feel supple and roll out easily without cracking.

14. Roll up the pastry onto the rolling pin and gently unroll over the tart ring.

15. Ease the pastry into the tin, taking care that there are no creases or cracks. Just smooth out any cracks or creases with your fingertips.

16. Do not trim the excess pastry but leave it overhanging. This ensures that the edge of the pastry will be still perfectly flush with the ring even if the shell shrinks. Reserve a little of the dough scraps for patching up the shell later.

17. Freeze the tart shell until very firm.

TO BLIND BAKE

18. Preheat the oven to 180°C (Gas 4).

19. Carefully line the chilled tart shell with foil, smoothing out any wrinkles and pressing the foil over the edges.

20. Fill with uncooked rice all the way to the top. I prefer to use rice instead of dried beans or baking weights because the rice creates a uniform mass that doesn't have any gaps.

21. Bake for 20 minutes for a large tart (or less for smaller tarts) or until the tart shell is golden brown all over.

22. Remove from the oven, then tip out the rice (allow to cool and use again as baking weights) and remove the foil. Return to the oven for 5 minutes to dry the pastry completely.

23. Remove from the oven and while the tart shell is still hot, patch up any holes or cracks with a smear of the reserved pastry scraps. You will only need to do this for large tart shells as they tend to crack.

24. While still hot, very lightly brush the potentially leaky parts of the shell or miniscule holes with the beaten egg yolk to seal. This is an important step if you are filling the tart with a liquid mixture. The tart shell is ready to use.

Pâte Sablée

This French-style shortbread or biscuit pastry, named after sand, is delicate, crumbly and buttery. It is "shorter" than the Pâte Sucrée (see page 34) because of its higher butter content, which means it's a little more difficult to handle. I find this shortbread incredibly moreish to eat, even on its own. I use it as a base for my Panna Cotta (see page 142) to add texture and it's also delicious layered with fruit, such as strawberries and cream, for a classic shortcake.

Makes 1.1 kg

400 g butter, softened (see page 28)
200 g caster sugar
1 egg yolk
25 ml thickened cream (35% milk fat)
500 g plain flour

MAKING THE DOUGH

1. Place the butter in the bowl of an electric mixer fitted with a paddle attachment. Work the butter slowly on low speed until smooth.

2. Add the sugar and mix together on medium speed until combined, taking care not to aerate it too much — you don't want it pale and fluffy.

EQUIPMENT
electric mixer
wooden spoon
sieve
palette knife or scraper
rolling pin
baking trays
pastry cutter

NOTE
• This pastry keeps well in the freezer for up to 1 month — just slice off the portion you need and thaw in the fridge overnight before using.

3. Remove the bowl from the electric mixer and add the egg yolk and cream.

4. Use a wooden spoon to incorporate into the butter mixture.

5. Sift the flour onto a work surface and make a well in the centre. Scrape the butter mixture in the flour well.

6. Using the tips of your fingers, work the butter mixture into the flour.

7. Keep working until the mixture resembles coarse breadcrumbs (see Note).

NOTE
- It's very important to not overwork the dough to ensure it remains tender and crumbly.

8. Using the heel of your hand, smear the mixture away from you until it looks smooth and no patches of butter remain.

9. Gather the pastry together with a palette knife or scraper to form a log (the diameter of the log will depend on how big you want your shortbread to be).

10. Wrap the log in plastic wrap. You will need to refrigerate for at least 2 hours to firm up, due to the high butter content.

TO BAKE

11. Preheat the oven to 160°C (Gas 2–3). Line a baking tray with baking paper.

12. Remove the pastry from the fridge. Remove the plastic wrap and cut the log into 7 mm thick slices. Place the slices on a work surface lightly dusted with flour.

Working with one slice at time, gently tap each slice with a rolling pin to soften the pastry, then roll out to a thickness of 3 mm.

13. Using a pastry cutter, cut out each slice to your desired size or shape. Slide a small kitchen knife under the pastry to dislodge the pastry from the surface.

14. Using the knife, carefully transfer the pastry disc onto the prepared tray. Remember this pastry is extremely fragile, so handle very gently. If the pastry breaks, just gently press the pieces back together. Don't reroll the scraps (see Notes).

15. Bake for 7 minutes or until just lightly golden around the edges. The tops should not be dark — think "shortbread" in colour.

Sablé Breton

This delicious pastry, originating in Brittany, is like a cross between shortbread and sponge cake due to the addition of baking powder. It requires less time to make than the other pastries as there is no chilling or resting involved. Just make and bake. I use it to make a tart base for my roasted fig and white chocolate mousse tart (see page 249) or it's delicious simply filled with Crème Pâtissière (see page 132) and berries. I also bake it into little biscuits and serve them as an accompaniment to my Rice Pudding (see page 219), or they would make a nice additon to the Crème Caramel (see page 265) too.

Makes 1.3 kg

160 g egg yolk (about 8)
350 g caster sugar
320 g butter, softened (see page 28)
440 g plain flour
15 g baking powder

EQUIPMENT
electric mixer
wooden spoon
sieve
rubber spatula
tart rings
baking tray

MAKING THE DOUGH

1. Place the egg yolk in an electric mixer fitted with a whisk attachment and begin whisking on high speed.

2. Sprinkle in the sugar in one batch and continue whisking until pale and creamy.

3. In a separate bowl, beat the butter until smooth.

4. Turn the speed right down and start adding the butter to the mixer, one-quarter at a time, whisking well between each addition but not so much as to deflate the yolk mixture.

NOTE
• The pastry is best baked immediately. You can freeze it, but form it first into a tart ring — thaw in the fridge before using.

5. Remove the bowl from the electric mixer. Sift in the flour and baking powder.

6. Using a rubber spatula, work slowly, gently folding in the flour until it is just combined.

7. Scrape the contents of the bowl onto a work surface and bring the dough together gently, making sure not to overwork it. The photo shows the texture you're aiming for. The pastry is now ready to use either to line tart rings or rolled out to make biscuits.

TO BAKE

8. Preheat the oven to 165°C (Gas 2–3). (Sablé Breton should be baked at a lower temperature than other pastry. This keeps it "blonde" and ensures that the delicate buttery texture and flavour are maintained.) Spray small tart rings with cooking spray and lightly dust with flour. Place on a baking tray lined with baking paper.

9. Gently press the pastry into the rings, pressing up the sides slightly to form a border.

10. Bake for 15–18 minutes (more for larger tarts) or until puffed up and golden brown. The pastry will sink slightly as it cools. Fill with your desired filling.

Puff Pastry

Take the time to try making puff pastry. Don't be afraid. It may take a few attempts to get it perfect, but when you do, it's so satisfying. The most important thing to remember is that the pastry should always be chilled before working it, otherwise it will shrink, lose shape or melt if too warm. The resulting buttery flaky pastry can be baked into decorated rounds (see page 67) or squashed into crisp shards as in my Mille-feuille (see page 256).

Makes 1.2 kg

400 g butter, softened (see page 28)
500 g plain flour, sifted
200 ml water
2 teaspoons cooking salt
2 teaspoons white wine vinegar
50 g butter, extra, melted
1 egg yolk, lightly beaten
   (only if making decorated rounds)

EQUIPMENT
sieve
rolling pin
pastry brush
pastry cutter
baking tray

MAKING THE DOUGH

1. Place the butter on a work surface and form into a slab, roughly 14 cm x 14 cm. (If using 250 g blocks, the best way to do this is to halve your blocks of butter lengthways, lay them next to each other, then bash out with a rolling pin.) Chill in the fridge until ready to use.

2. Tip the flour onto a work surface and make a well in the centre.

3. Pour the water, salt, vinegar and melted butter into the well. Work the ingredients in the well together using the fingertips of your one hand, while with your other hand, push small quantities of flour into the well as the mixture spreads out. (Use opposite hands if you're left-handed.)

4. When all the flour is mixed in well, lightly knead the dough for about 5 minutes until it is completely smooth. This dough is called the détrempe and it should be a very firm dough — don't worry, it will relax upon resting.

5. Roll the détrempe into a ball and cut a deep cross in the top to break the elasticity. Wrap the détrempe in plastic wrap and chill in the fridge for 2–3 hours.

6. Remove the détrempe from the fridge 1 hour before rolling.

7. Remove the slab of butter from the fridge about 30 minutes before rolling (see Notes).

8. Lightly dust a work surface with flour. Using the heel of your hand, push down firmly to create a flower shape. This will make rolling out the "ears" easier.

NOTES

- It is easier to make puff pastry when the room temperature is moderate. Too hot and the butter becomes too soft and will be squashed out of the détrempe when rolled. Too cold and it may crack and leave gaps in the layers.

- You need the butter and détrempe to be the same temperature before starting out.

8

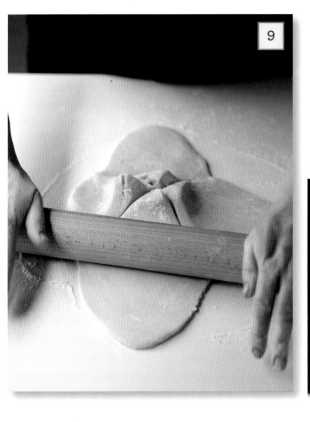

9. Using a rolling pin, roll out the dough to make four "ears" around the centre cross, making sure to leave a small mound of dough in the centre.

10. Always brush off the excess flour as you work as it will dehydrate the dough and you will have crusty layers in the final product.

11. Put the slab of butter in the centre of the détrempe. Give the butter a few whacks with the rolling pin to get rid of any air pockets and to get the two elements associated with each other.

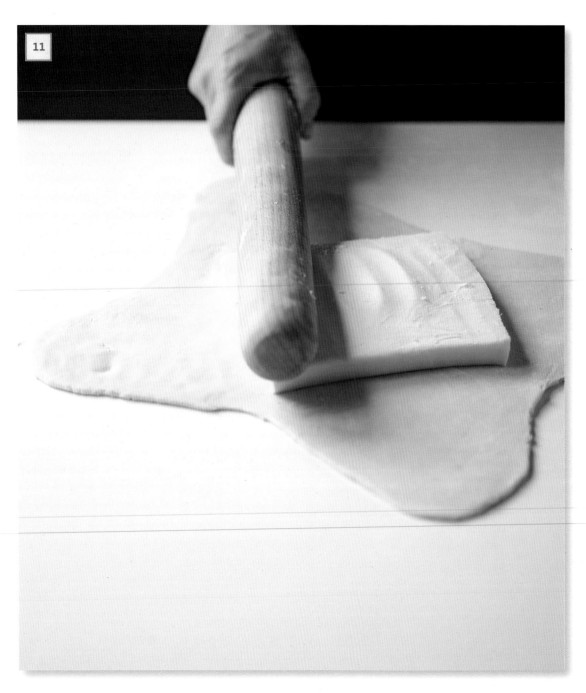

12. Fold up the four "ears" so the butter is completely enclosed, brushing any excess flour off each ear as you go.

13. Press the ears gently to seal.

14. Chill in the fridge for 30 minutes. This step ensures both the détrempe and butter will be the same temperature.

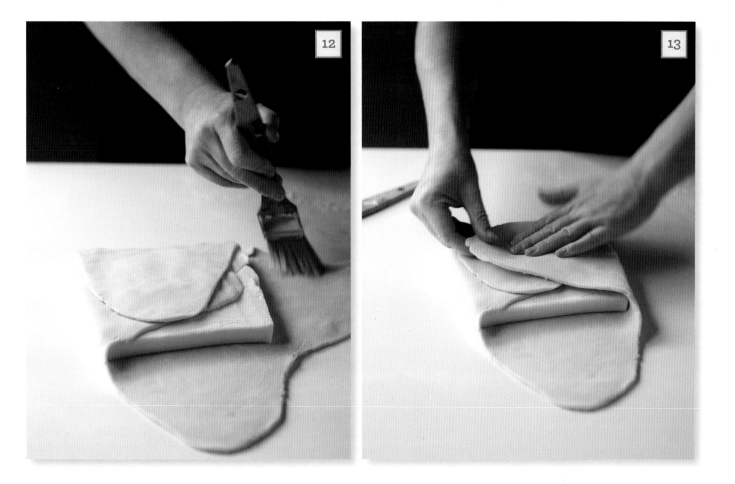

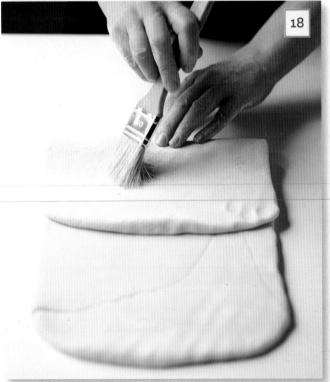

TURNING THE DOUGH

15. Remove the dough from the fridge
10–20 minutes before the next step.

16. Lightly dust a work surface with flour.
Give the dough several whacks with a rolling
pin to even it up and get things moving.
This makes it more malleable and easier to
roll out. Remember you want to keep the
top and bottom layers of the détrempe
the same size as the butter layer inside.

17. Progressively roll the dough away
from you to form a rectangle measuring
about 70 cm x 40 cm.

18. Mark out the dough into three equal parts.
Fold the third closest to you towards the centre,
then brush off the flour.

19. Then fold the top third over the centre and brush off the flour. This is called the first "turn".

20. Turn the rectangle 90 degrees clockwise.

21. Repeat rolling out the dough gently and progressively away from you, flouring the work surface as you roll, to form a rectangle measuring 70 cm x 40 cm. Fold the dough once more into three equal parts. This is the second turn.

22. At this stage, wrap the dough in plastic wrap and chill in the fridge for 30 minutes.

23. After chilling, give the dough two more turns, then chill for 30 minutes to 1 hour.

24. After chilling, give the dough two more turns, making it six turns in all. Chill again before rolling out according to the recipe or make decorated rounds as described overleaf.

NOTE
- Puff pastry is great to have on hand in the freezer. It keeps well for up to 2 months. Freeze it after the fourth turn and make sure you divide into four portions before freezing. Thaw in the fridge overnight before using, then continue making the final fifth and sixth turns.

ROLLING AND MARKING THE PASTRY

25. Roll out the chilled dough on a lightly floured work surface to 2 mm thick.

Cut out discs using a pastry cutter.

26. Remove the pastry discs from the cutter, brush off the flour and place upside down on a a cold, wet, heavy-based baking tray. Always turn the discs upside down as this frees up the layers of puff to rise. (The cold, wet tray ensures that the puff doesn't shrink or become misshapen during baking.)

27. Brush the discs with beaten egg yolk, taking care not to let the egg dribble down the sides as the puff will not rise properly.

28. Score the discs with the tip of a small sharp knife.

TO BAKE

29. Preheat the oven to 200°C (Gas 6).

Bake for 10–15 minutes or until puffed and golden.

Brioche

Brioche is a rich, buttery yeasted bread. I like to make the most of its buttery nature as a base in my Bread 'n' Butter Pudding (see page 214), where it transforms a classic comfort food from my childhood into an elegant dessert, or in the Pain Perdu (see page 244). This recipe makes a good amount of brioche, but I'm sure you'll find a use for it (and if not just store a loaf in the freezer).

Makes one large double loaf or four small single loaves

15 g fresh yeast (see Notes)
70 ml warm milk
6 eggs, at room temperature
500 g plain flour
15 g cooking salt
30 g caster sugar
350 g butter, softened (see page 28)
eggwash (see Notes)

> **NOTES**
> - Fresh yeast is available from bakeries and health food stores in the chilled section. You can substitute 10 g dried active yeast, added with the flour.
> - To make eggwash, beat 1 egg yolk with a dessertspoon of milk.

MAKING THE DOUGH

1. Put the yeast and milk in a bowl and lightly whisk to combine. Add the eggs.

2. Sift the flour and salt into the bowl of an electric mixer fitted with a dough hook attachment.

3. Pour the yeast mixture into the flour and knead on medium speed until the dough becomes smooth and elastic. This will take about 10 minutes.

4. Meanwhile, in a separate bowl, work the sugar into the butter until pale and creamy.

5. When the dough starts to come together as a lump on the hook and tears away from the side of the bowl, it's time to add the butter mixture.

EQUIPMENT
electric mixer
sieve
loaf tin/s
pastry brush
cooling rack

6. Start adding the butter mixture, about 2 tablespoons at a time, making sure that each addition is completely combined before adding more.

7. Once all the butter has been added, continue to mix for 5 minutes or until the dough is shiny and elastic.

8. Place the dough in a bowl and cover with plastic wrap. Leave at about 24°C for 2 hours.

9. After 2 hours, the dough should have doubled in volume. (If it hasn't, leave it to prove for a bit longer.)

10. Flip the dough over your fingertips a couple of times to knock it back.

11. This is how the dough should look after you have knocked it back. Cover with plastic wrap and refrigerate for several hours, but not more than 24 hours. This second proving is important as it firms the butter and makes the dough workable.

**MOULDING THE BRIOCHE
TO MAKE FOUR SMALL SINGLE LOAVES**

12. Lightly spray your loaf tins with cooking oil spray.

13. Place the dough on a work surface, dust lightly with flour and divide into four equal pieces.

14. Working with one piece of dough at a time, using your fist, punch down the dough.
Keep the other pieces covered with a tea towel.

15. Form the dough into a rectangular shape, about 2 cm thick and measuring 20 cm x 15 cm.

16. With one of the short edges closest to you, begin rolling up the dough.

17. Tuck in the edges as you go to prevent the pastry from blooming out when it proves.

18. Roll up to make a neat cylinder and push the seam together to seal.

19. This is your completed loaf. Place the loaf, seam side down, into the prepared tin.

20. Press the dough down firmly with your fist. Then, using your fingertips dipped in flour, push the edges of the loaf downwards. This ensures that the dough rises evenly and that there are no air pockets.

21. Lightly brush the loaf with the eggwash. Cover the loaf with a clean tea towel and leave at about 24°C until doubled in volume. This will take about 40 minutes at this temperature, but longer if cooler. Don't be tempted to place proving loaves somewhere warm to speed up the process as the butter may begin to soften or even melt and this could ruin the final result.

TO BAKE

22. Preheat the oven to 220°C (Gas 7). Lightly brush the proved loaf again with eggwash.

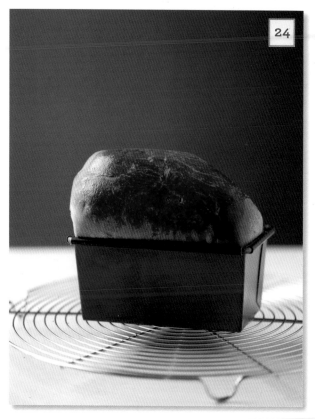

23. Bake the brioche for 20 minutes, then reduce the oven temperature to 190°C (Gas 5) and continue to bake for a further 20 minutes.

24. Cool the brioche in the tin briefly.

25. Unmould the brioche and cool on a cooling rack.

NOTE
- Brioche keeps well in the fridge, well wrapped, for several days or in the freezer for several months.

Cakes, Sponges & Meringue

Génoise

This versatile French sponge cake with its light-as-air texture is equally good split in half and filled with fruit and Crème Chantilly (see page 124) for a traditional teatime treat or broken up into pieces in my Tiramisu (see page 222). Don't be intimidated by baking a sponge cake — they're a lot more resilient than you think.

Serves 8

6 eggs
185 g caster sugar
180 g plain flour
40 g butter, melted

MAKING THE BATTER

1. Preheat the oven to 185°C (Gas 4–5). Lightly spray a 30 cm x 20 cm brownie tin or 22 cm diameter springfrom cake tin with cooking oil spray.

2. Select a saucepan that is wide enough to accommodate the base of the mixing bowl of an electric mixer. Fill it with water, bring to the boil, then reduce to a simmer.

3. Break the eggs into the bowl of an electric mixer fitted with a whisk attachment and whisk on high speed until pale and fluffy.

4. While whisking on high speed, gradually sprinkle in the sugar. Continue whisking until thick and foamy.

EQUIPMENT

springform cake tin
   or brownie tin
electric mixer
balloon whisk
digital sugar thermometer
sieve
rubber spatula
cooling racks

NOTE

- This cake is better made the day before because it will be less crumbly.

5. Remove the bowl from the electric mixer and place it over the pan of simmering water. Using a balloon whisk, whisk by hand.

6. Continue whisking until the mixture reaches 40°C. It will feel quite warm to the touch. This takes about 5 minutes. This stage stabilises the egg yolk.

7. Return the bowl to the electric mixer and continue to whisk on high speed until the mixture has cooled and holds soft peaks.

8. Remove the bowl from the electric mixer. Sift the flour over the egg mixture.

9. Using a rubber spatula, fold the flour through thoroughly, taking care not to deflate the mixture too much.

10. Add the butter and fold in gently until combined.

TO BAKE

11. Pour the batter into your prepared tin and bake for 15–20 minutes in a brownie tin or 20–25 minutes in a cake tin or until the top is golden brown and springy to the touch. To test if the sponge is cooked, insert a skewer into the centre; if it comes out clean, it's ready.

12. Immediately turn the cake out of its tin. To do this, place a cooling rack on top and carefully turn the cake out onto the rack to cool.

13. After 10 minutes, place another cooling rack on top of the cake and carefully flip the cake over onto the rack, so it's sitting on its base. The cake keeps well stored in an airtight container in the fridge for up to 3 days or well wrapped for several months in the freezer.

Biscuit Joconde

"Biscuit" means sponge or sandwich cake in French. Biscuit joconde is one of my favourite things (the other is Frangipane, see page 104) and I can't do without it in my kitchen. It is a lovely, supple almond sponge cake that can be manipulated and rolled as I do in my Almond Roly-Poly (see page 265). Almonds are typically used but you can also substitute hazelnuts or pistachios.

Makes a 60 cm x 40 cm slab

370 g TPT (see Frangipane, page 104)
5 whole eggs
150 g eggwhite
30 g caster sugar
60 g plain flour, sifted
40 g butter, melted and cooled

EQUIPMENT
heavy-based baking tray
silicone baking mat
electric mixer
hand-held electric beaters
sieve
rubber spatula
palette knife

MAKING THE BATTER

1. Preheat the oven to 220°C (Gas 7). Line a large heavy-based baking tray with a silicone baking mat or baking paper.

2. Place the TPT in the bowl of an electric mixer fitted with a whisk attachment.

3. Add the whole eggs and beat on high speed until pale and thick.

NOTE
- This malleable cake is delicous rolled up with berries and Crème Chantilly (see page 124) or layered with Chocolate Mousse (see page 148).

4. In another bowl, whisk the eggwhite, using hand-held electric beaters, until white and foamy and the whisk leaves a faint trace.

5. Reduce the speed, sprinkle in the sugar and continue whisking until the eggwhite mixture holds "soft peaks" (see page 23).

6. Add one-third of the eggwhite mixture to the TPT mixture along with the sifted flour and cooled melted butter.

7. Using a rubber spatula, fold the ingredients together thoroughly. This will loosen the batter and make it easier to fold in the remaining eggwhite mixture without deflating it.

8.–10. Then add the remaining eggwhite mixture and gently fold in. Begin with the spatula in the middle of the bowl, touching the bottom, and move outwards towards yourself. Turn the bowl anticlockwise as you make the motion. Keep gently folding and turning until the eggwhite mixture is completely incorporated.

11. Pour the batter onto the baking mat or into the prepared tray.

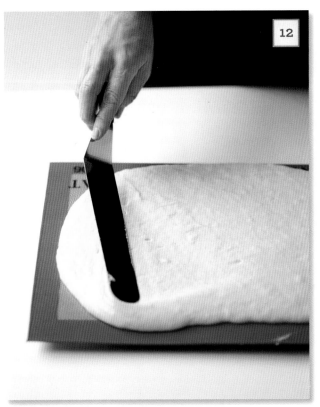

12. Use a palette knife to spread the batter to an even thickness of about 1.5 cm.

TO BAKE

13. Bake for 5 minutes or until just springy to the touch and lightly golden on top. Slide the cake and baking mat or paper off the tray to cool completely.

14. Trim the edges of the cake so you have a neat rectangle.

15. Turn the cake upside down onto a piece of baking paper and gently peel off the baking mat or paper. Use as directed in the recipe.

Chocolate Sponge Cake

This is a delicate cake that contains no flour. Like the Biscuit Joconde, it is made with whisked whites and the method is the same (see pages 83–93 to follow the steps). I use it as the base for mousse cakes and include it in my Tiramisu (see page 222) for a rich and decadent touch. It is also delicious rolled up with Crème Chantilly (see page 124) and the fruit of your choice.

Makes a 60 cm x 40 cm slab

250 g best-quality dark couverture
    (see page 26), finely chopped
    or grated (or use buttons)
60 g butter, cubed
60 g egg yolk (about 3)
250 g eggwhite
80 g caster sugar

MAKING THE BATTER

1. Preheat the oven to 180°C (Gas 4). Line a large heavy-based baking tray with a silicone baking mat or baking paper.

2. Finely chop or grate the chocolate and melt in a heatproof bowl over a saucepan of barely simmering water. Let more than half of the chocolate melt before you give it a stir with a wooden spoon or rubber spatula.

3. When the chocolate has melted, turn off the heat and add the butter. Stir to combine and keep warm.

4. In another bowl, whisk the egg yolk with a fork.

EQUIPMENT
heavy-based baking tray
silicone baking mat
heatproof bowl
heatproof rubber spatula
    or wooden spoon
electric mixer
palette knife

NOTE
- This cake is best used on the day of baking. You can freeze it for up to 1 month, wrapped well in plastic wrap.

5. Place the eggwhite in the bowl of an electric mixer fitted with a whisk attachment. Whisk until white and foamy and the whisk leaves a faint trace.

6. Reduce the speed, sprinkle in the sugar and continue whisking until the eggwhite mixture holds "soft peaks" (see page 23).

7. Add one-third of the eggwhite mixture to the chocolate mixture along with the yolks. Using a rubber spatula, fold the ingredients together thoroughly. This will loosen the batter and make it easier to fold in the remaining eggwhite mixture without deflating it.

8. Then gently fold in the remaining eggwhite mixture.

9. Pour the batter onto the baking mat or the prepared tray. Use a palette knife to spread the batter to an even thickness of about 1.5 cm.

TO BAKE

10. Bake for 8–10 minutes or until just springy to the touch. Slide the cake and baking mat or paper off the tray to cool completely.

11. Trim the edges of the cake so you have a neat rectangle. Turn the cake upside down onto a piece of baking paper and gently peel off the baking mat or paper. Use as directed in the recipe.

Dacquoise

A crisp yet chewy nutty meringue that is a lot like a macaron. I use it as the base for my Snickers (see page 253). The beauty of this meringue is that you can substitute hazelnuts or pistachios or even coconut for the peanuts for a simple twist. All variations are lovely bases for mousses: hazelnuts with dark chocolate mousse and raspberries, or pistachios with white chocolate mousse and roasted apricots are irresistible combinations.

Makes a 40 cm x 25 cm slab

180 g roasted peanuts
50 g almond meal
1 teaspoon cooking salt
250 g icing sugar, sifted
160 g eggwhite
100 g caster sugar

EQUIPMENT
heavy-based baking tray
silicone baking mat
food processor
electric mixer
sieve
rubber spatula
palette knife

MAKING THE BATTER

1. Preheat the oven to 180°C (Gas 4). Line a large heavy-based baking tray with a silicone baking mat or baking paper.

2. In a food processor, grind the peanuts with the almond meal and salt. Tip into a bowl, add the icing sugar and thoroughly mix.

3. Place the eggwhite in the bowl of an electric mixer fitted with a whisk attachment. Whisk until white and foamy and the whisk leaves a faint trace.

4. Sprinkle in the caster sugar and continue whisking on high speed until the meringue is shiny and holds firm peaks (see Notes).

NOTES

• The dacquoise needs to be used on the day of baking. Do not store in the fridge or it will become sticky. However, you can also freeze it, wrapped well in plastic wrap.

• Due to the high ratio of sugar to eggwhite, this meringue is very stable and difficult to overbeat.

5. Remove the bowl from the mixer, add the nut and icing sugar mixture and quickly but gently fold together.

6. Fold together thoroughly but take care not to overwork the mixture.

7. Scrape the dacquoise onto the baking mat or the prepared tray.

8. Use a palette knife to spread the dacquoise to an even thickness of about 1 cm.

TO BAKE

9. Bake for 15–20 minutes. It should be firm and crisp on top and lightly golden but still gooey in the centre. Slide the cake and baking mat or paper off the tray and leave to cool completely.

10. Turn the dacquoise upside down onto a piece of baking paper and gently peel off the baking mat or paper. Use as directed in the recipe.

French Meringue

French meringue is a crisp, light meringue. The key to its dissolve-on-your-tongue airiness is whisking the eggwhite and sugar to the correct stage. This is a fundamental skill (and easy too once you know what signs to look for) that creates a cake or dessert's voluminous "oomph". I use French meringue to make the angel wings for my Snow White and Rose Red (see page 240). Or you could easily pipe the meringue into dainty discs to serve as petits fours.

Makes 18 angel wings or 18 x 3.5 cm rounds

100 g eggwhite, at room temperature
160 g icing sugar, sifted

BEATING THE EGGWHITE

1. Preheat the oven to 90°C. (You want your oven at this low a temperature because you are essentially dehydrating the meringue rather than baking it). Line a large heavy-based baking tray with a silicone baking mat or baking paper.

2. Place the eggwhite in the bowl of an electric mixer fitted with a whisk attachment. Add 1 heaped tablespoon of the icing sugar.

EQUIPMENT
heavy-based baking tray
silicone baking mat
electric mixer
piping bag (optional)

NOTE
- Due to the high ratio of sugar to eggwhite, this meringue is very stable and difficult to overbeat. But always keep an eye on it in the mixer. Don't walk away!

3. Whisk the whites until the mixture holds "soft peaks". You should still be able to make out bubbles in the mixture.

4. Add the remaining icing sugar. Continue whisking at high speed until the meringue is shiny and holds "firm peaks", also called a "bird's beak".

5. The meringue is now ready to use. Pipe or spoon desired shapes onto the prepared tray.

TO BAKE

6. Bake for 1 hours 45 minutes (for 3.5 cm rounds) or until crisp and dry (but you don't want them to turn pinky brown). You will need to bake larger or high meringues for longer. Remove from the oven and cool on the tray.

NOTE
- The baked meringues must be stored in an airtight container away from humidity.

Frangipane

This is a pastry chef's staple — versatile and simple. Traditional frangipane owes its distinct flavour to almonds ground with sugar. If you want to flavour up your frangipane, you can easily replace some of the almond with other types of nuts such as pistachios and hazelnuts. I use it as a filling in my Fruit Tartlets (see page 216). It can also be baked as a shallow cake.

Makes 500 g (enough to fill 1 large tart or 8 mini tarts)

125 g butter, softened (see page 28)
25 g plain flour, sifted
250 g TPT (see Notes and recipe below)
2 whole eggs
1 egg yolk

TPT
500 g almond meal
500 g pure icing sugar

EQUIPMENT
food processor
sieve
electric mixer
whisk
rubber spatula

MAKING THE TPT
1. Pulverise the almond meal in a food processor, then sieve. Combine with the icing sugar, measure out 250 g and freeze the remainder.

MAKING THE BATTER
2. Place the butter in the bowl of an electric mixer fitted with a paddle attachment. Work the butter until smooth.

3. Add the TPT and continue beating until very pale and fluffy.

NOTES
- TPT is abbreviated French for "tant pour tant" which means "quantity for quantity". It stores well in the freezer, so I like to make 1 kg at a time.
- To make other nut flavours, simply replace half of the almond meal in the TPT with finely ground hazelnuts or pistachios.

4. In a bowl, whisk the eggs and egg yolk together with a fork. While beating, add the whisked egg, a little at a time, to the butter mixture, making sure each addition is incorporated before adding more. When all of the whisked egg is incorporated it should look smooth and creamy.

5. Remove the bowl from the electric mixer and fold in the flour using a rubber spatula.

6. The frangipane is now ready to use, for example to fill tart rings to make tart shells. Remember to not fill the frangipane all the way to the top as it will rise during baking. Bake as directed in recipes.

NOTE

- The frangipane can be stored in an airtight container in the fridge for up to 1 week. Bring to room temperature before using.

Doughnuts

These dainty little doughnuts are mouth-poppingly addictive, especially when still hot and simply rolled in sugar. Of course, you can fancy these gems up with a dusting of fragrant cinnamon sugar, fill them with Crème Pâtissière (see page 132) for the ultimate custard bombs or, if you want to go all out, soak them in a spiced sugar syrup as I do on page 262.

Makes about 20

220 ml milk

40 g butter, softened (see page 28)

6 g fresh yeast (see Note)

2 whole eggs

1 egg yolk

300 g plain flour, sifted

40 g caster sugar, plus extra for dusting

¼ teaspoon cooking salt

vegetable or canola oil, for deep-frying

EQUIPMENT
sieve
whisk
piping bag
rubber bands
thermometer
    (or wooden spoon)
scissors
slotted spoon

MAKING THE DOUGH

1. Warm the milk in a small saucepan over low heat. Add the butter and stir until melted. Remove from the heat and allow to cool to blood temperature.

2. Crumble the fresh yeast into a small bowl and add a little of the cooled milk mixture. Set aside for the yeast to soften and begin to activate.

NOTE
- Fresh yeast is available from bakeries and health food stores in the chilled section. You can you substitute 4 g dried active yeast, added with the flour.

3. Whisk the whole eggs and egg yolk in a large bowl and add the yeast mixture and remaining milk mixture.

4. Combine the flour, sugar and salt in a large bowl and make a well in the centre.

5. Add the wet ingredients and, using a sweeping stroke with your hand, work together until smooth. This will take several minutes (see Notes).

6. The dough is ready when it feels stretchy and elastic.

7. Put the mixture into a large piping bag (as it needs to accommodate the expanding dough) fitted with a small plain nozzle and secure each end with a rubber band. Leave the dough to prove at room temperature until doubled in volume. This will take about 1½ hours (see Notes).

NOTES

- I prefer to mix the dough by hand as it's the best way to get a feel for the dough and not to activate the gluten in the flour too much.

- You can also leave the dough to prove in the fridge overnight (it will take about 12 hours) instead of at room temperature.

TO COOK

8. In a saucepan, heat the oil to 180°C or until the handle of a wooden spoon bubbles vigorously when dipped in.

9. Using scissors dipped in the hot oil, begin snipping off walnut-sized blobs of the dough straight into the oil. Dip the scissors into the oil in between every snip. Make 8–10 doughnuts at a time, so the oil doesn't reduce in temperature too much.

10. The doughnuts should roll over on their own when they're cooked on one side, but if they don't, use a slotted spoon to flip them over. They should take about 4 minutes to cook through but, just to be sure, test one by breaking it in half.

11. When the doughnuts are ready, remove with the slotted spoon and drain on kitchen paper.

12. Roll the doughnuts in sugar while still hot and enjoy warm.

Brownies

An old favourite that I never tire of. Chocolatey, fudgey brownies win hearts all over. And they are very easy to make. You can go traditional as I've done here, or for speckled brownies, vary the additions. Add nuts like pecans or macadamias or milk and white chocolate, or even rum-soaked raisins for a grown-up version. I crumble the brownie and add it to vanilla ice-cream to finish off my Raspberry and Chocolate Délice (see page 261).

Makes a 30 cm x 20 cm slab

300 g best-quality dark couverture
    chocolate (see page 26),
    finely chopped or grated
200 g butter, cubed
4 eggs
200 g caster sugar
80 g soft brown sugar
1 teaspoon vanilla extract (optional)
200 g plain flour
1 teaspoon baking powder
80 g best-quality dark couverture
    chocolate, extra, roughly chopped
    (see Notes)

EQUIPMENT
brownie tin
heatproof bowl
heatproof rubber spatula
    or wooden spoon
electric mixer
sieve

NOTES
*   You can replace the chunks of dark chocolate with a different type of chocolate or the same quantity of chopped nuts, or a combination of both.

1. Preheat the oven to 180°C (Gas 4). Line a 30 cm x 20 cm brownie tin with baking paper.

2. Finely chop or grate the chocolate and melt in a heatproof bowl over a saucepan of barely simmering water. Let more than half of the chocolate melt before you give it a stir with a wooden spoon or rubber spatula.

3. When the chocolate has melted, turn off the heat and add the butter. Stir to combine and keep warm.

4. In the meantime, place the eggs in the bowl of an electric mixer fitted with a whisk attachment and lightly whisk.

5. Add both the sugars and whisk until pale and creamy. Add the vanilla extract and fold through.

6. Fold the egg mixture into the warm chocolate mixture.

7. Sift over the flour and baking powder and fold through. Stir through the roughly chopped chocolate.

8. Pour into the prepared tin and bake for 15–20 minutes or until slightly puffed and springy to the touch. The brownie should be shiny and slightly cracked on the surface. Allow to cool in the tin before turning out.

Gingerbread

Whenever I smell this baking, it's like Christmas in the house. The honey is an alluring background note to all the spices and the orange zest gives the cake a lift. I crumble it up and use it to make my Gingerbread Ice-cream (see page 262).

Makes a 30 cm x 20 cm slab

250 g honey
150 g plain flour
100 g rye flour
1 teaspoon ground cinnamon
a pinch of ground nutmeg
1 teaspoon ground ginger
finely grated zest of 1 orange
20 g baking powder
3 eggs
125 ml milk
50 g caster sugar
½ teaspoon vanilla extract

EQUIPMENT
brownie tin
digital sugar thermometer
sieve
whisk
cooling rack

MAKING THE BATTER

1. Preheat the oven to 160°C (Gas 2–3). Line a 30 cm x 20 cm brownie tin with baking paper or spray with cooking oil spray.

2. Warm the honey in a saucepan over low heat until completely liquid, then cool to about 25°C.

NOTE
- This gingerbread is delicious served plain or spread with a little butter and jam for afternoon tea.

3. Sift the flours together into a large bowl. Add the spices, orange zest and baking powder, stir to distribute evenly, then make a well in the centre.

4. In a separate bowl, whisk the eggs, milk, sugar and vanilla extract together.

5. Pour the cooled honey and the egg mixture into the flour mixture and whisk to form a smooth, elastic batter.

5

6. Pour the batter into the prepared tin.

TO BAKE

7. Bake for 40 minutes or until dark golden on top. To test if it's cooked, use the tip of a knife. If the knife comes out clean, the cake is ready.

8. Allow to cool in the tin for 10 minutes before turning out onto a cooling rack to cool completely.

NOTE

- **Store the cake in the fridge, well wrapped in plastic wrap, for several days, or freeze for up to 1 month.**

Creams & Mousses

Whipped Cream and Crème Chantilly

I use thickened cream for all the recipes in this book. Thickened cream contains 35 per cent milk fat and gelatine. Cream varies from country to country. Sometimes thickened cream is referred to as "whipping cream". Just check the fine print on the label to make sure you're using the right cream. I use plain whipped cream to incorporate into things, such as my Chocolate Mousse (see page 148), parfait mixtures or Crème Pâtissière (see page 132). Whereas Crème Chantilly, with its slightly sweetened edge, is luscious dolloped on just about anything, especially cakes, tarts and fruit.

Makes 500 g (enough to serve 6–8 as an accompaniment)

Whipped Cream
500 ml thickened cream (35% milk fat),
  or your desired amount, chilled
  (see Notes)

EQUIPMENT
whisk or electric mixer
sieve

1. Make sure the bowl you use is cold. (If it's a hot day, it's a good idea to chill the bowl in the fridge.) Pour the cream into the bowl.

NOTES

- Always make sure cream is well chilled before using to reduce the chances of it splitting and curdling.

- It is best to whip cream close to you when you need to use it, but whipped cream will store well in the fridge, covered with plastic wrap.

2. Whisk the cream by hand or in an electric mixer fitted with a whisk attachment until it starts to form a "ribbon" when the whisk is lifted. Continue to whisk carefully for another 30 seconds or until the cream holds very "soft peaks". It is now ready to use as directed in the recipe.

Crème Chantilly

50 g icing sugar, sifted
1 teaspoon vanilla extract, or to taste (optional)
500 ml thickened cream (35% milk fat)

1. Add the sugar and vanilla to the cream.

2. Follow the instructions for Whipped Cream.

3. Continue to whisk past the "soft peak" stage for 2–3 minutes or until the cream holds its shape and is "spoonable" but still soft (see Note). It is now ready to use.

NOTE

- Take care to not over-whisk the cream or it will turn to butter. If you're using an electric mixer, don't turn your back on it!

Crème Anglaise

Crème anglaise is basically custard. It may seem old fashioned to make your own custard but it is an essential part of a pastry chef's artillery. From these four basic ingredients of milk, cream, sugar and egg yolks, pure magic happens. It adds a decadent finishing touch when served as a sauce to accompany simple fresh berries or a luxe dessert (like my Summer Pudding on page 227), it's the building block to any good ice-cream (see page 134), and I like to use an under-sweetened or "base anglaise" to make my Chocolate Mousse (see page 148).

Makes 650 ml

250 ml milk
250 ml thickened cream (35% milk fat)
100 g caster sugar (see Notes)
100 g egg yolk (about 5)

EQUIPMENT
whisk
wooden spoon
sugar thermometer (optional)
sieve

1. Combine the milk and cream in a saucepan and bring to a simmer.

2. In a large bowl, whisk the sugar into the egg yolk until pale and thick (see Notes).

3. Pour one-third of the hot milk mixture into the egg yolk mixture, whisking constantly. This "tempers" or stabilises the egg yolk. If you add all the hot liquid at once, the yolks could "shock" and curdle.

NOTES

- If making a base crème anglaise, omit 50 g of the caster sugar.

- Egg yolks "burn" if left in contact with sugar. The burning causes little nodules that are impossible to get rid of and will spoil the result, so don't be tempted to add the sugar to the yolk until the milk mixture is hot and ready to go. And make sure you whisk them together immediately.

4. Pour the egg yolk mixture back into the pan and place over medium heat. Stir constantly but gently and slowly with a wooden spoon, using a figure-eight movement until the mixture begins to thicken and the bubbles disappear.

5. The crème anglaise is ready when, if you lift the wooden spoon from the mixture and draw a line with your finger across the back of it, the line remains distinct without liquid running into it for several seconds. If you are unsure, use a thermometer and when the temperature reaches 80°C, it's ready.

6. Pour the crème anglaise into a bowl and place it over a larger bowl half-filled with iced water to arrest the cooking. You will notice a slightly "scrambled" appearance on the base of the pan. This indicates the crème anglaise is cooked properly. Stir the anglaise regularly as it cools.

7. Once cooled, strain through a sieve. It is ready to serve or use as directed in the recipe.

NOTE

• **You can store the crème anglaise in the fridge for several days.**

Crème Pâtissière

This is a delicious, unctuous cream thickened with cornflour to add more body than Crème Anglaise (see page 126). It's also known as pastry cream, and its extra heft means that it holds up well as a filling in cakes, eclairs and profiteroles. I like to fold through a little Whipped Cream (see page 122) for a decadent addition to fruit tarts or use it to lighten my Rice Pudding (see page 219).

Makes about 750 g

300 ml milk
225 ml thickened cream (35% milk fat)
100 g caster sugar
½ vanilla bean, halved and seeds scraped
  (optional)
15 g cornflour
60 g egg yolk (about 3)

1. Combine the milk and cream in a saucepan. Add half of the sugar and the vanilla bean and seeds and bring to a simmer.

2. In a large bowl, whisk the remaining sugar and all of the cornflour into the egg yolk until pale and thick.

EQUIPMENT
whisk
sieve

NOTES

• Unlike crème anglaise, pastry cream needs to come back to a simmer to cook the cornflour. The addition of the cornflour prevents the egg yolk from scrambling so there's no need to worry about over-cooking.

• You can store the crème pâtissière in the fridge for up to 1 week.

3. Strain a little of the hot milk mixture through a sieve into the egg yolk mixture, whisking constantly. Continue straining in the milk mixture, bit by bit, and whisking.

4. Pour the mixture back into the pan. Place over medium heat and bring to a simmer (see Notes), whisking all the time until the crème pâtissière is thick and shiny.

5. Remove from the heat and keep whisking as it cools. It is now ready to use. If not using immediately, press a piece of plastic wrap directly onto the surface or dust with pure icing sugar to prevent a skin from forming (see Notes).

Ice-cream

Nearly all of my favourite desserts involve an ice-cream or sorbet or both. Nothing beats the texture of a freshly churned silky ice-cream as an accompaniment to either fresh fruit, such as berries, or poached fruit. And, of course, ice-cream with a hot dessert like a crumble is divine. An ice-cream machine is a great investment and worth its benchspace. Don't be intimidated by making your own ice-cream. It is really as easy as making a Crème Anglaise (see page 126), infusing it with whatever you desire, then churning it. If time is an issue, you can always make the anglaise the day before and churn it when you're ready.

Vanilla Ice-cream
500 ml milk
500 ml thickened cream (35% milk fat)
2 vanilla beans, halved and seeds scraped
200 g caster sugar
200 g egg yolk (about 10)

MAKING THE CRÈME ANGLAISE

1. Follow the steps to make a crème anglaise on pages 126–130 using the quantities given above.

2. Add the vanilla bean and seeds to the milk and cream in step 1. Chill the mixture until ready to churn (see Notes).

CHURNING THE ICE-CREAM

3. Churn the mixture in an ice-cream machine according to the manufacturer's instructions (see Notes). If not serving immediately, store in the freezer. Makes 1.5 litres.

EQUIPMENT
whisk
wooden spoon
digital sugar thermometer
   (optional)
sieve
ice-cream machine

NOTES

- You can refrigerate the crème anglaise at this stage for up to 3–4 days and churn when you're ready.

  Always churn ice-cream no more than several hours before you're ready to serve, if possible. If it becomes too firm, place in the fridge to soften a little just before serving.

- Take care not to over-churn the ice-cream or it will become buttery and spoil the texture.

Lemon Verbena Ice-cream

500 ml milk

500 ml thickened cream (35% milk fat)

200 g egg yolk (about 10)

200 g caster sugar

finely grated zest of 1 lime (rubbed
into the sugar; see pages 176–7)

2 handfuls fresh lemon verbena leaves
(see Note, opposite)

MAKING THE CRÈME ANGLAISE

1. Follow the steps to make a crème anglaise on pages 126–130 using the quantities given above, up to the end of step 5.

2. Place the verbena leaves in a bowl. When the anglaise has reached 80°C, strain the anglaise over the lemon verbena and leave to infuse for 30 minutes, stirring regularly.

3. Strain again, then chill the mixture until ready to churn (see Notes, page 134).

CHURNING THE ICE-CREAM

4. Churn the mixture in an ice-cream machine according to the manufacturer's instructions (see Notes, page 134). If not serving immediately, store in the freezer. Makes 1.5 litres.

Rose Geranium Ice-cream

500 ml milk

500 ml thickened cream (35% milk fat)

200 g caster sugar

200 g egg yolk (about 10)

6–8 rose geranium leaves, roughly torn
(see Note, below)

MAKING THE CRÈME ANGLAISE

1. Follow the steps to make a crème anglaise on pages 126–130 using the quantities given above, up to the end of step 5.

2. Place the rose geranium leaves in a bowl. When the anglaise has reached 80°C, strain the anglaise over the rose geranium and leave to infuse for 30 minutes, stirring regularly.

3. Strain again, then chill the mixture until ready to churn (see Notes, page 134).

CHURNING THE ICE-CREAM

4. Churn the mixture in an ice-cream machine according to the manufacturer's instructions (see Notes, page 134). If not serving immediately, store in the freezer. Makes 1.5 litres.

> **NOTE**
>
> - Rose geranium imparts a lovely fragrance to ice-cream and custards. It is an easy shrub to grow. It's available in nurseries, or for those with a foraging heart, look for them in front yards. Keep in mind that there are many types — you want to pick one that smells "rosy".
>
>   If you can't find rose geranium, use rosewater to taste instead.

Gingerbread Ice-cream

1 litre milk
500 ml thickened cream (35% milk fat)
1 vanilla bean, halved and seeds scraped
1 cinnamon stick
25 g caster sugar
150 g honey
300 g egg yolk (about 15)
250 g gingerbread (see page 116)

MAKING THE CRÈME ANGLAISE

1. Combine the milk, cream, vanilla bean and seeds and cinnamon in a saucepan and bring to a simmer.

2. In a large bowl, whisk the sugar and honey into the egg yolk.

3. Pour the hot milk mixture into the egg yolk mixture, whisking constantly.

4. Pour the mixture back into the pan and place over medium heat. Stir constantly with a wooden spoon using a figure-eight movement until the mixture coats the back of the spoon (see page 128) or reaches 80°C.

5. Remove from the heat and allow the anglaise to infuse for 15 minutes.

6. Crumble the gingerbread into a large bowl, then strain the anglaise over the gingerbread.

7. After several minutes or once the gingerbread has softened, use a stick blender to blitz the mixture until smooth.

8. Chill the mixture until ready to churn (see Notes, page 134).

CHURNING THE ICE-CREAM

9. Churn the mixture in an ice-cream machine according to the manufacturer's instructions (see Notes, page 134). If not serving immediately, store in the freezer. Makes 2 litres.

6

Quenelles

Traditionally quenelles (which refers to any mixture shaped into an "egg") were formed using two spoons but these days, for a more organic seamless shape, most chefs use this one-spoon method. You can form anything from ice-cream and sorbet to mousse and cream into quenelles. To get quenelles right, you will need to put in some practice; left-over whipped cream or sorbet is ideal for practising as they can be rechurned.

1. You will need a spoon (the size depends on how big you want to make the quenelle) and a container of very hot water to dip your spoon into. When the spoon is hot, dip it into your mixture, with the rounded bottom facing you.

2. Push the spoon away for a brief length, then carefully flip the rounded bottom of the spoon back towards you.

3. The mixture should curl up on itself forming a nice egg shape. Remember to work quickly as the spoon mustn't cool down too much or the mixture will stick and ruin the smooth effect you are aiming for.

4. For sorbets and ice-creams, a good trick is to rub the bottom of the spoon with the palm of your hand for several seconds. This conducts heat through the metal, which facilitates the mixture slipping off and gives it a nice shine.

5. Always re-dip the spoon in hot water between each quenelle. Serve immediately.

Panna Cotta

This is one of the simplest and most crowd-pleasing desserts there is. I describe panna cotta (which means "cooked cream" in Italian) as a creamy milk jelly. It's a great dessert to add to your dinner-party repertoire because you can make it ahead of time (it actually tastes better if you do), forget about it while it sets, then pull it out when the time is ready. And it's easy to infuse this basic recipe with different flavours. My favourite variations are on page 144.

Makes 10

4 gold-strength gelatine leaves (8 g)
  (see Note)
750 ml thickened cream (35% milk fat)
300 ml milk
160 g caster sugar
1 vanilla bean, halved and seeds scraped

MAKING THE PANNA COTTA

1. Soak the gelatine in iced water until softened. (If you are using powdered gelatine, place in a small bowl and mix with 2 teaspoons of cold water to soften.)

EQUIPMENT
wooden spoon
125 ml capacity dariole
  moulds

NOTE

- Gelatine comes in several forms. I use gold strength and as a general rule one leaf equals 2 g, so if you only have, for example, titanium-strength leaves or powdered gelatine, you can substitute 1 gold-strength leaf with 2 g of whatever type of gelatine you have.

  I tend to shun powdered gelatine as I find its flavour unpleasant.

  Gelatine leaves are available from good supermarkets, specialty food suppliers or online.

2. In a saucepan, combine the cream, milk and sugar and vanilla bean and seeds. (Add your choice of flavourings at this stage, if applicable; see Variations, below.) Stir and bring to a simmer.

3. Squeeze the excess water from the gelatine and stir into the hot cream mixture. (If using powdered gelatine, just add the mixture to the pan as is.) Stir over low heat until the gelatine has completely dissolved, then remove from the heat.

4. If you have infused a flavour into the panna cotta, for example vanilla or cinnamon, allow the mixture to sit for 10 minutes

VARIATIONS

- **Honey Panna Cotta**

  Omit 80 g of the sugar and the vanilla bean. Add 70 g honey to the pan when heating the cream mixture in step 2.

- **Pistachio and Cinnamon Panna Cotta**

  Omit 50 g of the sugar and the vanilla bean. Add 30 g pistachio paste and a cinnamon stick to the pan when heating the cream mixture in step 2.

- **Mascarpone or Yoghurt Panna Cotta**

  Omit 400 ml of the cream. Add 400 g mascarpone or yoghurt to the mixture after straining in step 5.

5. Strain the mixture into ten 125 ml capacity dariole moulds (see Notes).

6. Refrigerate for 4 hours or preferably overnight.

TO SERVE

7. To turn out the panna cottas, dip each mould into very hot water and give it a little shake. Turn the mould upside down onto a plate or a pâte sablée biscuit (see Notes) and shake gently to dislodge. It should have a nice wobble.

NOTES

- I prefer to use metal dariole moulds as it is easier to turn the panna cotta out, but plastic moulds are fine too.
- I like to turn my panna cottas onto pâte sablée discs (see page 44) to add a crunchy element and a touch of elegance.

Chocolate Mousse

This is my favourite way of making chocolate mousse. I use a slightly under-sweetened crème anglaise as the base, which makes it smooth and velvety rather than dense or airy. I use milk chocolate mousse in my Snickers dessert (see page 253) and a white chocolate version in my Fig Tart (see page 249). But this is equally delicious with just a dollop of Crème Chantilly (see page 124).

Makes about 1 kg

your choice of best-quality couverture
   chocolate (see Variations), finely
   chopped or grated
300 ml base crème anglaise
   (see Notes, page 126)
450 g whipped cream (soft peak stage)
   (see page 124)

EQUIPMENT
heatproof bowl
wooden spoon
heatproof rubber spatula
digital sugar thermometer

1. Melt the chocolate in a large heatproof bowl placed over a saucepan of barely simmering water. Let more than half of the chocolate melt before you give it a stir with a wooden spoon or rubber spatula.

2. You want the temperature of the melted chocolate to be about 45°C.

3. Carefully warm the crème anglaise to about the same temperature as the chocolate, so that when they are mixed the chocolate doesn't seize up. This is important as the chocolate will set and become unworkable if the anglaise is too cold. (If you are using white chocolate, add the softened gelatine to the anglaise when warm and stir to dissolve.)

VARIATIONS

* **Dark Chocolate Mousse**
  Use 400 g dark chocolate.

* **Milk Chocolate Mousse**
  Use 500 g milk chocolate.

* **White Chocolate Mousse**
  Use 500 g white chocolate. You will
  need to add 4 gold-strength gelatine
  leaves (8 g) (see page 142). First
  soften them in iced water, then
  squeeze out the water and add
  when heating the crème anglaise.

4. Add one-third of the warm anglaise to the melted chocolate.

5. Using a rubber spatula, begin stirring the two together just in one section of the bowl to form a core of mixture (as if you were making a mayonnaise) — you are not mixing everything together. This will ensure that the chocolate doesn't split.

6. Add half of the remaining anglaise, gradually working in more of the chocolate.

7. Now add the remaining anglaise and mix thoroughly until the mixture is smooth and shiny and looks almost elastic.

7

CREAMS & MOUSSES ✦ 151

8. While the chocolate is still very slightly warm, add one-third of the whipped cream and quickly fold through with the spatula.

9.–10. Allow to cool for several minutes, then fold through the remaining whipped cream. Make sure the cream is completely incorporated.

11. The mousse is now ready to use. Spoon into serving glasses or use to fill dessert rings.If you would like to quenelle the mousse (see page 140), first refrigerate it for several hours — the mousse will firm up as the chocolate sets.

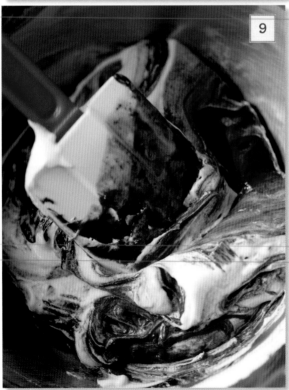

NOTE
• If the mousse has
been refrigerated
and you don't want
to make quenelles,
bring it up to room
temperature before
eating — chocolate
tastes richer if it's
not too chilled.

Fruit

Poaching

Choosing the correct ripeness of fruit for poaching makes all the difference to the result. Take pears, for example. You want to choose one that is not too hard but not too ripe either. Whereas for stone fruit, like peaches, you want to choose a specimen at its perfect peak of ripeness.

Poaching Orchard Fruits

4–5 orchard fruits, such as pears
   or apples
500 g caster sugar
1 litre water

CHOOSING THE RIGHT PEAR

1. When choosing pears for poaching, pick fruit that is "in between" hard and ripe. Ripe fruit will become soft and squishy when poached, whereas ripe fruit will stay hard and discolour. The picture opposite shows the perfect "in between" pear for poaching in the middle, while the pear on the left is too ripe and the pear on the right is too hard. You want to choose the one that is just right. I always buy slightly under-ripe green pears and let them ripen for several days before poaching.

MAKING THE POACHING SYRUP

2. Choose a wide-based saucepan that will accommodate the fruit, in this case pears, fairly snugly without squashing it. Combine the sugar and water in the pan and bring to the boil, stirring to dissolve the sugar. Reduce the heat to a simmer.

EQUIPMENT
small melon (parisian) scoop
peeler
slotted spoon

NOTES
- As a general rule, if you want to double the quantity of fruit for poaching, double the quantity of poaching syrup too.
- Poached pears feature in my Poire Belle-Héllène on page 237.

PREPARING THE FRUIT

3. Use a melon (parisian) scoop to remove the core of the pears from the base, taking care to get out all the seeds. Snip the stalks at an attractive length.

4. Starting at the stalk and moving downwards, carefully peel the skin with a peeler.

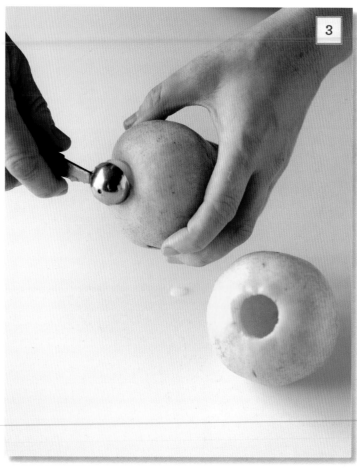

TO POACH

5. Add the fruit to the simmering poaching syrup and increase the heat. Cover the surface with a cartouche (see Note, page 160), pressing the baking paper directly onto the surface, then place a plate on top to ensure the fruit stays submerged.

6. When the syrup comes back to the boil, reduce the heat so it is just simmering. Gently poach for about 15 minutes or until you can easily pierce the flesh with the tip of a knife.

7. Allow the fruit to cool in the syrup, covered with the cartouche, then refrigerate in the syrup until needed. The pears will keep in the fridge for up to 1 week, but make sure they are submerged in the syrup.

NOTE

- To make a cartouche:
1. Fold a sheet of baking paper large enough to fit your saucepan in half crossways, then in half again lengthways, then in half into a triangle.
2. Trim the triangle so that it is the same length as the radius of your pan.
3. Snip the tip off the triangle to create a hole for the steam to escape.
4. Open out the triangle. (You can always cheat and trace around your saucepan, then cut the circle out.)

Poaching Stone Fruits

3 perfectly ripe stone fruit, such as
  peaches, nectarines, apricots or plums
300 g caster sugar
1 litre water

PREPARING STONE FRUIT

1. If you are using peaches or nectarines, but not apricots or plums, you need to remove their skins first (see Notes, below). Bring a pot of water to a rapid boil and have a bowl of iced water at hand

2. Cut the fruit in half, following its natural line around. Gently twist to separate the halves without bruising the flesh. Remove the stones.

3. Plunge the peaches or nectarine halves into the water for 20 seconds, then, using a slotted spoon, gently remove anzd drop into the iced water. Slip off their skins and discard.

MAKING THE POACHING SYRUP

4. Follow the instructions on page 156 to make the poaching syrup, using the quantities given above.

NOTES
- The peaches or nectarines need to be perfectly ripe or their skins won't slip off ... Very frustrating!
- I poach peaches to use in my Peach Melba for Oprah on page 232.

TO POACH

5. Carefully add the fruit halves, cut side up, to the simmering poaching syrup. Cover the surface with a cartouche (see Note, opposite), pressing it onto the surface.

6. Gently poach. As the fruit is ripe for eating, the poaching won't take long (not more than 10 minutes). You're not aiming to "cook" the fruit per se, but you're essentially hot-marinating it. Flip the fruit over to ensure the cut sides don't discolour, then remove from the heat.

7. Allow the fruit to cool in the syrup, then refrigerate in the syrup until needed. The fruit will keep in the fridge for up to 1 week, but make sure it is submerged in the syrup.

Poaching Dried Fruits

300 g dried fruit, such as prunes,
  apricots and figs
350 g caster sugar
1 litre water

1. Soak the dried fruit (separately if you are using different types) in hot water for several hours or until plump and moist, then drain.

2. Follow the instructions on page 156 to make the poaching syrup and poach the fruit, using the quantities given above, but poach the fruit for about 1 hour or until it is swollen and soft.

3. Allow the fruit to cool in the syrup, then refrigerate in the syrup until needed. The fruit will keep in the fridge for up to 1 week, but make sure it is submerged in the syrup.

Disgorging

Disgorging is a technique used to extract moisture from fruit and vegetables while infusing flavour at the same time. It is most commonly done to rhubarb. I toss the rhubarb with sugar and aromatics and the sugar draws out the moisture while the aromatics permeate the rhubarb. If you don't disgorge rhubarb that you plan to bake or poach, it will end up pulpy. The action of disgorging ensures the rhubarb will hold its shape and remain firm. I bake disgorged rhubarb in my Snow White and Rose Red dessert (see page 240).

5 medium-thick stalks of rhubarb
caster sugar (amount depending on
   trimmed weight of rhubarb)
3 rose geranium leaves, roughly torn
   (see Note)
½ vanilla bean, halved and seeds scraped

PREPARING THE FRUIT

1. Peel the rhubarb stalks using a small sharp knife — strip the fibrous outer membrane off in long strands as you would for celery.

NOTES

- Rhubarb is technically a vegetable but I've included it in this chapter because you use it in sweets as you would other types of fruit.
- Rose geranium imparts a lovely floral fragrance. It is a very easy shrub to grow. It's available in nurseries, or for those with a foraging heart, look for them in front yards. Keep in mind that there are many types — you want to pick one that smells "rosy". If you can't find rose geranium, use rosewater to taste instead.

2. Cut the stalks into 4 cm lengths.

3. Weigh the rhubarb; for every 100 g of rhubarb, use 50 g of caster sugar.

DISGORGING

4. Toss the rhubarb and sugar together. At this stage, you can also toss the fruit with any flavourings you like. In this example, I like to use rose geranium leaves and vanilla bean and seeds.

5. Leave to "disgorge" for 20 minutes, stirring regularly. Bake the disgorged rhubarb and its juices as directed in the recipe.

Juices and Jellies

Pure fruit juices (or essences) should be clear and full of flavour — think of them as sweet "consommés". The most successful juices come from pulpy or watery fruit such as strawberries or other berries. Flavoursome, ripe seasonal fruits, such as peaches or pears, work well too, but the fruit must be distinctively fragrant and tasty or the juice will just taste of sweet water. One of my favourite things to do with a pure fruit juice is to make a jelly. Or just drizzle the juice over fruit for an extra layer of intense flavour (like I do in my Snow White and Rose Red dessert on page 240).

Pure Fruit Juice
1 kg sliced perfectly ripe fruit or frozen
   berries (except strawberries; see Notes)
100 g caster sugar

1. Prepare your fruit and weigh to yield 1 kg.

2. Toss with the sugar and leave to "disgorge" (see page 162) for several hours. If using frozen berries, combine the fruit with the sugar, then allow to defrost in a warm place, stirring occasionally until all the juice is released.

3. Put the fruit mixture in a sieve lined with muslin placed over a large bowl to drain.

4. Allow the juice to drain naturally without pressing down on the solids. The key to a perfectly crystal clear juice is to not push down on the solids to extract the liquids otherwise the sediment may make the juice cloudy.

5. Discard the pulp and refrigerate the juice until needed. Makes 200–500 ml, depending on the juiciness of your fruit.

Jelly
100 ml pure fruit juice, at room
   temperature
1 gold-strength gelatine leaf (2 g),
   softened in iced water, then squeezed
   to remove excess water (see Notes)

1. Heat 50 ml of the juice over low heat. Add the gelatine and stir until dissolved. Remove from the heat.

2. Add the remaning room temperature juice to the hot liquid, then strain into a container. Refrigerate until set.

EQUIPMENT
sieve
muslin

NOTES
- For berries, such as raspberries and blackberries, you will get more yield if the fruit is frozen.
- One leaf of gold-strength gelatine to 100 ml of liquid will give a firmly set jelly. If you prefer your jelly a little more wobbly, just add some more juice. I generally use 9 gelatine leaves for every 1 litre of juice if I want to get a wobble on.

Sorbet

Sorbets are my pride and joy. When I first started making sorbet, I used the sugar syrup/Baume measurement method to varying degrees of success. Over the years, I have developed this chart. Using the quantities given in the chart, and following my method, will result in perfect sorbet every time. The chart is all about balance, so that the fruit shines through without being too sweet or too icy.

Sorbet chart

FRUIT	CASTER SUGAR (per 1 kg fruit)	POWDERED GLUCOSE	WATER
Strawberry *	225 g	75 g	nil
Rockmelon *	250 g	70 g	100 ml
Honeydew melon *	250 g	70 g	50 ml
Watermelon *	240 g	70 g	nil
Apricot **	300 g	85 g	285 ml
Peach **	260 g	75 g	95 ml
Pear **	300 g	60 g	300 ml
Lemon or lime ***	600 g	360 g	1360 ml
Orange ***	225 g	35 g	nil
Mandarin ***	225 g	45 g	nil
Grapefruit ***	225 g	65 g	nil
Raspberry ***	260 g	50 g	120 ml
Blackberry ***	250 g	50 g	120 ml
Mango ***	360 g	100 g	540 ml
Passionfruit ***	360 g	170 g	470 ml
Pineapple ***	300 g	80 g	280 ml

Strawberry/Rockmelon/ Honeydew Melon/ Watermelon Sorbet *

1. Weigh hulled strawberries or peeled chunks of melon to yield 1 kg.

2. Purée the fruit, in this case strawberries, with the sugar, glucose (and water if applicable) in a blender until a smooth purée forms.

3.–4. Strain the purée through a sieve, using a spoon to push the mixture through.

5. Churn in an ice-cream machine according to the manufacturer's instructions, then freeze for 1–2 hours or until firm.

EQUIPMENT
blender
sieve
ice-cream machine
rubber spatula
loaf tin or take-away
   container (for freezing)
citrus juicer
piping bag
palette knife

NOTE
- **Powdered glucose is readily available at supermarkets, chemists and health food shops.**

NOTE
- **Some fruits benefit from cooking and some definitely do not. Melons, for example, will taste soapy if heated and strawberries will taste jammy when cooked. On the other hand, pears and apricots need to be cooked to enhance their flavour and to prevent the fruit from discoloring and tasting pulpy or watery. Of course, the results are dependent on the quality of the fruit. Sub-standard fruit makes sub-standard sorbet.**

Apricot/Peach/Pear Sorbet **

1. Peaches and pears need to be peeled, but not apricots. Halve the fruit and remove the stones or cores, then weigh the prepped fruit to yield 1 kg.

2.–3. Combine the fruit, in this case apricots, with the sugar, glucose and water in a heavy-based saucepan and simmer until the fruit is tender (see Note).

4. Purée the fruit in a blender until smooth. Strain the purée through a sieve, using a spoon to push the mixture through. Allow to cool.

5. Churn in an ice-cream machine according to the manufacturer's instructions, then freeze for 1–2 hours or until firm.

NOTE
• You can add flavourings, such as a split and scraped vanilla bean, at this stage to the sorbet — just make sure you remove it before you purée the mixture.

Citrus/Raspberry/Blackberry/Mango/ Passionfruit/Pineapple Sorbet ***

1. If using berries (see Note), mangoes passionfruit or pineapples, purée in a blender first. Weigh the purée or juice to yield 1 kg.

2. Combine half of the purée or juice, in this case blackberry purée, with the sugar, glucose (and water if applicable) in a heavy-based saucepan. Bring to the boil, stirring regularly with a whisk to ensure the sugar has dissolved.

3. Cool, then add to the remaining purée or juice.

4. Churn in an ice-cream machine according to the manufacturer's instructions, then freeze for 1–2 hours or until firm.

NOTE
- **If making a raspberry or blackberry sorbet, frozen berries work very well.**

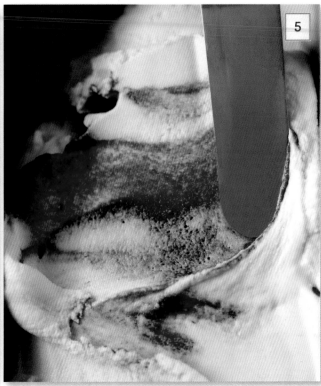

Blackberry and Yoghurt Sorbet

350 ml milk
140 g caster sugar
70 g trimoline or liquid glucose (see Note)
500 g full-cream plain yoghurt
juice of 1 lemon, strained
½ quantity blackberry sorbet, unchurned
  (see page 173)

1. Combine the milk, sugar and trimoline or liquid glucose and bring to the boil. Allow to cool completely, then whisk in the yoghurt and lemon juice.

2. Churn in an ice-cream machine according to the manufacturer's instructions. Store in the freezer in a loaf tin or take-away container, covered, while you churn the blackberry sorbet.

3. Churn the blackberry sorbet and freeze in a separate container for up to 1 hour, depending on your freezer. Both sorbets should be firm but still malleable.

4. Put the blackberry sorbet into a piping bag and pipe at 3 cm intervals into the yoghurt sorbet.

5. Smooth the top with a palette knife. If there are peaks and troughs, then the surface will freeze unevenly. Press a piece of plastic wrap onto the surface to cover and store in the freezer until needed.

NOTE
• Trimoline is a super-
saturated sugar syrup
(an invert sugar).
You can buy it online
or at specialty food
suppliers. Liquid glucose
is readily available
from supermarkets and
is an okay substitute
for trimoline.

Zesting and Segmenting Citrus

Citrus fruits are the jewels of winter. They are the support act to so many of my desserts. The zest and the juice play different roles, adding fragrance, sweetness and acid to both savoury and sweet dishes. Rubbing the zest into the sugar boosts the citrus flavour tenfold because the precious oils are absorbed by the sugar.

Rubbing Zest Into Sugar
caster sugar (amount depends on recipe)
your choice of citrus fruit, washed
   (see Note)

1. Place the sugar in a bowl. Use a fine Microplane grater to remove the zest from the citrus. Grate the zest directly into the bowl with the sugar to catch all the oils. Don't apply too much pressure or you will remove some of the bitter pith when all you want is the surface of the skin that contains the oil and fragrance.

2. Rub the zest into the sugar using the tips of your fingers.

3. The sugar absorbs the oils and takes on the flavour and colour of the zest. It is ready to use as directed in the recipe.

NOTE
• Always choose brightly coloured fruit when using the zest and don't forget to wash them, otherwise, if they have been in contact with another mouldy citrus, the mould may linger and impart an off odour to your dishes.

EQUIPMENT
Fine Microplane

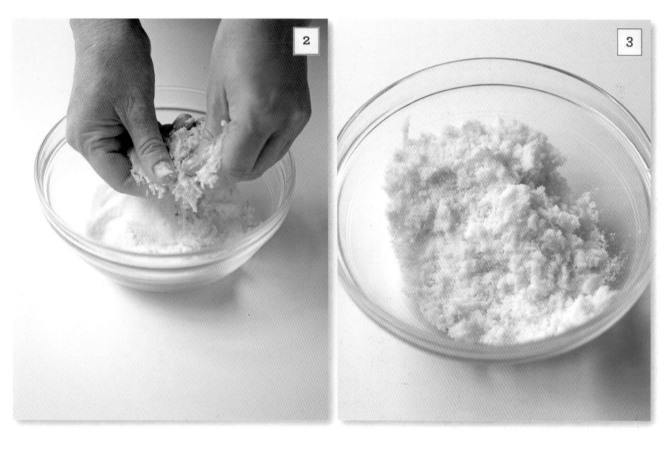

Segmenting Citrus

your choice of citrus fruit

1. Use a super sharp knife to remove the skin and white pith from the fruit, slicing with smooth, firm strokes from the top to the base.

2. Segment the citrus by sliding the knife between the dividing membrane. If your knife is not very sharp, you will tear the little nobules that hold the juice and you will end up with raggedy segments.

NOTE
- **Segment the fruit as close to serving as you can, so they retain their gloss, freshness and juiciness.**
- **Use a very sharp knife so you don't damage the segments.**

Confit Citrus Zest

This is essentially candied zest. The sugar balances out the bitterness of the pith and softens the zest. Always use brightly coloured oranges or lemons for the most attractive results. I like to make thin strips of zest and also cut out small rounds of zest to make candied "pearls" to use as a garnish on my mille-feuille (see page 256).

3–4 oranges or lemons (see Note)
300 ml sugar syrup (see below)

Sugar Syrup
250 g caster sugar
300 ml water

EQUIPMENT
peeler
small melon (parisian) scoop
(optional)
sieve

1. Combine the sugar and water in a saucepan and bring to the boil, stirring to dissolve the sugar. Reduce the heat to a simmer.

2. Thoroughly wash and dry the citrus fruit. Using a peeler, remove the zest in large strips.

3. With a very sharp knife, remove any excess pith.

NOTE
- **Always confit different types of citrus zest separately, otherwise they will end up tasting the same.**

4. Cut each piece of zest into thin strips. Using a small melon (parisian) scoop, cut out circles from the remaining zest to make "pearls".

5. Put all the zest in a small saucepan and barely cover with cold water. Bring to the boil, then drain through a sieve.

6. Repeat this process twice more. (This removes the bitter oils.)

7. Return the drained, blanched zest to the pan and cover with the sugar syrup.

8. Cook on the lowest possible heat with just barely a bubble breaking the surface. Cover the surface with cartouche to keep the zest submerged. If it floats to the top it will crystallise. Cook for about 1 hour or until the zest is transparent and glossy. Cool in the syrup before using.

NOTE
- Store the zest in its syrup at room temperature or in the fridge, for up to several months.

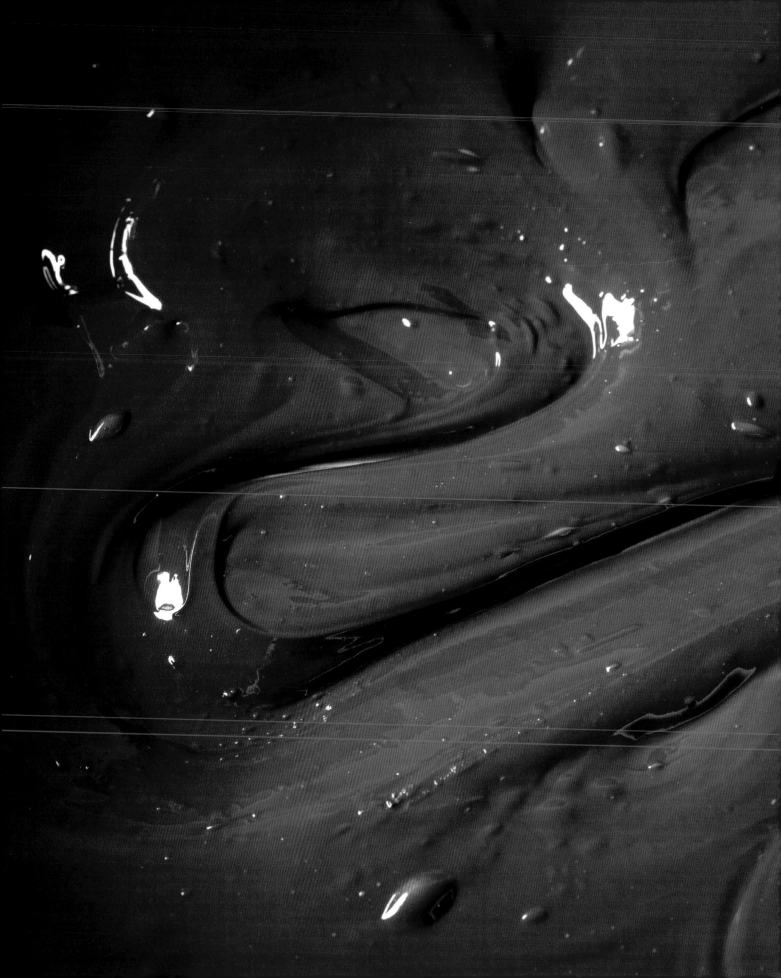

Chocolate Work & Garnishes

Tempering Chocolate
Chocolate Decorations
Nut Pralines and Candied Nuts
Crystallised Petals

Tempering Chocolate

Tempering chocolate sounds like a daunting task but it's all about temperature. When chocolate is heated and melted the fat molecules separate and to reunite them you need to temper the chocolate, which stabilises the molecules and ensures it sets with a wonderful sheen and crack. Chocolate work should be done at room temperature, ideally between 18°C and 24°C. If it is too hot, then the chocolate won't set; if it's too cold, then it sets so quickly you won't have time to work with it. Humidity can cause problems as well. I temper chocolate for dipping, moulding and for the plaques for my Snickers (see page 253) and the Raspberry Chocolate Délice (see page 261).

your choice of best-quality dark couverture, milk or white chocolate (see page 26)

EQUIPMENT
heatproof bowl
wooden spoon or heatproof
  rubber spatula
digital sugar thermometer
large step-palette knife or
  pastry scraper

MELTING CHOCOLATE

1. Finely chop or grate the chocolate (see Notes) and melt in a heatproof bowl over a saucepan of barely simmering water. Let more than half of the chocolate melt before you give it a stir with a wooden spoon or rubber spatula.

2. Remove from the heat and stir until smooth and shiny. The temperature of the chocolate should be 50–55°C for dark couverture, no more than 50°C for milk chocolate and no more than 45°C for white (see Notes).

NOTES

- When chopping or grating chocolate, try to get it as fine as possible as it will be much easier to melt and be lump-free.

- Due to the higher sugar and cocoa butter content in milk and white chocolate, they are far more delicate and more likely to be ruined if they get too hot.

2

TEMPERING CHOCOLATE

3. Pour two-thirds of the chocolate onto a cool work surface (marble and stainless steel are the best). Set aside the remaining chocolate and put back on the pan of simmering water off the heat to keep warm.

4.–5. Using a large step-palette knife or scraper, work the chocolate continuously, bringing it up over itself.

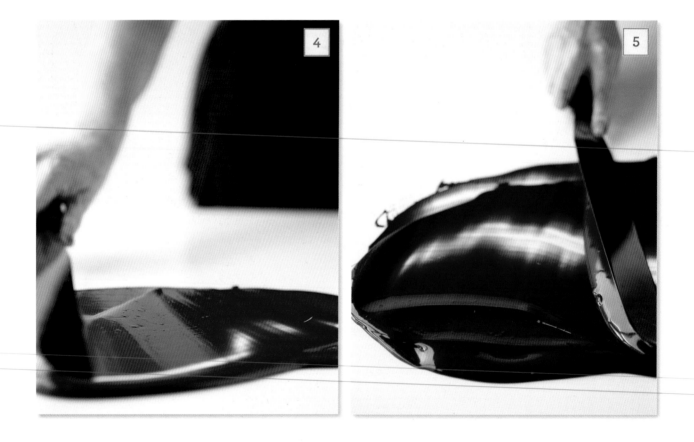

6. Keep working the chocolate until it begins to thicken and the temperature drops to 26°C.

7. Scrape the chocolate off the work surface and return it to the bowl with the remaining warm chocolate.

8. Stir the chocolate until it reaches 30–32°C for dark and milk chocolate, and 28–29°C for white chocolate. The tempered chocolate is now ready to use.

Chocolate Decorations

Chocolate curls, cigarettes and plaques make for lovely light garnishes
that complement and add a little theatre to chocolate desserts and cakes. It might
take some time to master but keep practising. For curls and cigarettes, you don't
have to go to the trouble of tempering the chocolate, while plaques are well worth
the effort for their wow factor and the "crack" that they add to desserts when you
bite into them. The great thing about working with chocolate is that if you do
make a mistake you can just scrape it all up and re-use it! You can make all of
these ahead of time and pull them out when you need to end the night with
a flourish.

Chocolate Curls

200 g dark, milk or white chocolate,
    in block form at room temperature

EQUIPMENT
small metal pastry cutter

1. Using a small metal pastry cutter, scrape
the surface of the chocolate towards you
at a slight angle so only part of the edge
of the cutter scrapes against the chocolate.

2. The chocolate will naturally curl up inside
the cutter. If the chocolate is too cold and
doesn't curl up, rub the surface with the
palm of your hand to warm it up slightly. Keep
the curls in a sealed container in the fridge or
freezer until needed.

NOTE
- I use white chocolate
  curls to decorate my
  Sablé Breton with
  Roasted Figs, White
  Chocolate Mousse and
  Port (see page 248).

3

EQUIPMENT
large roasting or baking tray
large step-palette knife
scraper

Chocolate Cigarettes

200 g best-quality dark couverture
  chocolate (see page 26)

1. Follow the steps to melt the chocolate
on page 186, then allow to cool to 35°C.

2. Heat a large, clean, heavy-based roasting
tray or baking tray in a 180°C (Gas 4) oven.
Remove after several minutes and place upside
down on a work surface. Allow to cool until you
can leave the palm of your hand on the surface
for 5 seconds. This ensures the chocolate will
spread evenly and not set straight away.

3. Spread the chocolate evenly over the tray
using a large step-palette knife. The layer
should be about 0.5 mm thick or as thin
as you can get it.

4. Now place the tray in the fridge for about
10 minutes or until set.

5. Remove the tray from the fridge and leave
at room temperature for several minutes.

6. Using a scraper, push the chocolate away
from you using short rapid movements. The
chocolate should roll into slender cigarettes.
Leave them on the tray. If the chocolate
crumbles or cracks, it needs to sit at room
temperature for longer. If it doesn't curl up but
rather comes off the tray in sheets, it has become
too warm and needs to be returned to the fridge
to firm up a little.

7. Once you have made the cigarettes, return
the tray to the fridge until the cigarettes have
hardened. They can then be gently removed
from the tray.

8. Keep the cigarettes in a sealed container
in the fridge or freezer. Makes about 20.

Chocolate Plaques

200 g best-quality dark or milk couverture
  chocolate (see page 26)

1. Follow the steps to melt and temper the
chocolate on pages 186–9 and cool to 30–32°C.

2. Cut the sheet of acetate just a bit larger than
your desired measurements. Use masking tape
to stick the strips of acetate onto a work surface,
leaving a few millimetres between each.

3. Pour the tempered chocolate onto
the strips of acetate.

4. Spread the chocolate with a large step-
palette knife over the strips of acetate to
about 1.5 mm thick. Leave to set at room
temperature.

EQUIPMENT
sheet of acetate
  (see Note below)
masking tape
scissors
large step-palette knife

NOTES

- These beautiful, shiny, crisp
  plaques add a satisfying snap to
  my Snickers (see page 253) and
  Raspberry and Chocolate Délice
  (see page 261). They are also a
  wonderful decoration on cakes
  and mousses.

- Acetate is flexible transparent
  plastic film and is available
  from craft or specialty
  kitchenware stores.

5.–6. When the chocolate has set to the touch but is still slightly malleable, peel the strips off the surface.

7. Place the strips upside down onto a clean surface, so that the chocolate is face down. Place a tray on top to prevent the chocolate from warping as it hardens at room temperature.

8. To trim the plaques so that the edges are neat and flush, mark the chocolate with a knife heated under hot water, then cut the acetate with scissors.

9. Keep the plaques in a sealed container in the fridge or freezer. Leave the acetate on the plaques until you are ready to peel them to serve.

Nut Pralines and Candied Nuts

Pralines are nuts coated with caramelised sugar while candied nuts are crunchy sugary bliss bombs. Both make a lovely addition to ice-creams and I like to use them to top my Crème Cassonade (see page 212) instead of actually "brûlée-ing", for extra crunch and flavour.

Praline

150 g hazelnuts (see Notes)

150 g caster sugar

30 ml water

1. Preheat the oven to 160°C (Gas 2–3). Line a baking tray with baking paper.

2. Spread the nuts on the baking tray and roast for 5–10 minutes or until the skins begin to loosen.

3. Rub the skins off the nuts by rubbing them in a tea towel.

4. Roughly chop or crush the nuts using a mortar and pestle.

EQUIPMENT
baking tray
mortar and pestle (optional)
pastry brush
wooden spoon
digital sugar thermometer

NOTES

- You can use most nuts to make pralines or candies: almonds, pistachios, hazelnuts, walnuts, cashews or pecans all work well.

- You can also leave the nuts whole if you prefer (as I do for the my almond praline in my Sauternes Crème Caramel, Thyme-Roasted Apricots and Almond Roly-Poly on page 265). Use two forks to separate the hot nuts in step 9 when you pour them onto the tray to cool.

5. Return the nuts to the baking tray to reheat later.

6. Put the sugar and water in a saucepan over medium heat and stir with your fingers until dissolved a little, then brush any crystals down from the side of the pan using a pastry brush dipped in cold water.

7. Cook the syrup, without stirring, over medium–low heat until it starts to colour.

8. Put the nuts back in the oven briefly to heat them up.

9. Continue cooking the syrup, swirling the pan gently, until golden.

10. Tip in the nuts and stir to coat with a wooden spoon.

11. Pour onto the prepared tray, spreading out evenly with a wooden spoon, and allow to cool completely before using.

12. You can break the praline into large pieces, roughly crush using a mortar and pestle or finely grind. Store well in an airtight container in the freezer (not the fridge, as it will become sticky) for up to 3 weeks.

Candied nuts

150 g almonds (see Notes, page 196)

100 g caster sugar

100 ml water

1. Preheat the oven to 160°C (Gas 2–3). Line a baking tray with baking paper.

2. Roughly chop or crush the nuts using a mortar and pestle to the size you want, or leave them whole if you like.

3. Put the sugar and water in a saucepan over medium heat and stir with your fingers until dissolved a little, then brush any crystals down from the side of the pan using a pastry brush dipped in cold water.

4. Bring to the boil over medium heat and allow to bubble away undisturbed, without stirring or shaking the pan, until the syrup reaches 118°C.

5. Put the nuts in the oven to warm up.

6. When the syrup reaches 121°C, tip in the warm nuts.

7. Stir with a wooden spoon for several minutes until the syrup forms a candy coating around the nuts and sounds dry and crunchy.

8. Pour onto the prepared tray, spreading out evenly with a wooden spoon, and allow to cool completely before using. You can break it into large pieces, roughly crush using a mortar and pestle or finely grind. Store well in an airtight container for up to 2 weeks.

Crystallised Petals

These beautiful, crisp and fragrant garnishes add a touch of glamour and elegance to a plate. It's important to use roses that have not been sprayed with chemicals. Always check with your florist first. Choose the most beautiful, unblemished petals you can find. And a word of warning: if it's a humid day, forget about trying to make these. I use the petals on my Snow White and Rose Red dessert (see page 240). I also use yellow rose petals to decorate my Sauternes Crème Caramel (see page 265).

rose petals of your choice

eggwhite

caster sugar

EQUIPMENT
cooling rack

1. Using your fingertips, gently paint a very thin layer of eggwhite over both sides of the petal. They should be just wet but not too wet or they will appear lumpy and unattractive.

NOTE

- These crystallised petals don't store for long so it is best to prepare them no more than a day in advance. Keep in a dry place (not in a sealed container) until needed.

2. Carefully roll the petals, in batches of three, in the sugar.

3. Shake off any excess sugar and place on a cooling rack.

4. Leave in a cool, dry place to harden and crisp up. This will take several hours, depending on the humidity.

Recipes

Classics

Lemon Tart

Crème Brûlée or
Crème Cassonade

Bread 'n' Butter Pudding

Fruit Tartlets

Rice Pudding with
Poached Fruits

Tiramisu

Summer Pudding

Lemon Tart

The lemon tart has a simplicity of flavour and texture that has made it a classic.
The sucrée tart shell makes for a soft, buttery pastry case that just melts in the mouth. I
like to serve this on its own, but you can add a dollop of cream or top with Confit Citrus
Zest (see page 180) for extra indulgence.

Serves 8—10

Tart shell
½ quantity (550 g) pâte sucrée
   (see page 44), chilled
1 egg yolk, lightly beaten

Filling
300 g caster sugar
finely grated zest of 3 lemons
   (see Note, page 210)
9 eggs (450 g)
250 ml strained lemon juice
250 ml thickened cream
   (35% milk fat)

To serve
pure icing sugar, for dusting

FOR THE TART SHELL

Preheat the oven to 180°C (Gas 4). Line a baking tray with
baking paper and place a 20 cm-diameter x 4 cm-deep dessert
ring on top.

Follow the instructions on pages 38–41 to work the pâte sucrée
and roll out to line the ring. Freeze the tart shell until very firm.

FOR THE FILLING

Rub the lemon zest into the sugar to release the oils (see
page 176). Whisk the eggs together with the lemon zest and
sugar mixture until foamy. Stir in the lemon juice, then the
cream, and set aside for the proteins to begin breaking down
while you blind bake the tart shell.

TO BLIND BAKE THE TART SHELL

Remove the tart shell from the freezer and line carefully with
foil. Make sure the foil is flush with all the surfaces of the pastry.
Remember any creases or spaces will result in faults in the shell.

Fill the shell all the way to the top with uncooked rice and fold
the foil down around the edge of the ring. Bake the shell for
about 20 minutes.

Flick the foil upwards and pull gently to release the steam. Bake
for a further 10 minutes or until light golden brown.

Remove the foil and rice carefully and return to the oven. Reduce
the oven temperature 130°C (Gas 1) and continue baking until
the tart shell is dry and golden brown all over.

Remove the shell. If there are any cracks, use a little of the
pastry scraps and the beaten egg yolk to patch them up
while the tart shell is still hot (see pages 42–3). ⟶

TO BAKE THE FILLING

Whisk the filling briefly and skim off any big bubbles. Return the shell to the oven and with the door open, pour the filling into the shell right to the top. Carefully close the oven door and bake undisturbed for 50 minutes.

Check the tart by very gently wobbling the tray. If the filling still seems liquid, give the tart another 5-10 minutes.

Once cooked, cool the tart for 10 minutes before trimming the overhanging pastry from the rim. Allow it to cool completely before lifting off the ring. Sprinkle with icing sugar and serve.

NOTE
- Always wash citrus fruits before zesting. Citrus fruits can taste mouldy if they are not washed.

Stressed spelled
backwards
is desserts.
Coincidence?
I think not.

UNKNOWN

Crème Brûlée or Crème Cassonade

Everyone is familiar crème brûlée but for something different, instead of caramelising sugar for a glaze, I like to top the cream with a crunchy praline. I call this a crème cassonade because the praline topping resembles coarse sugar or "casson". Make these up to three days ahead for a stress-free dessert.

Makes 10 small

1 litre thickened cream
  (35% milk fat)
180 g caster sugar, plus extra for
  sprinkling, if caramelising
1 vanilla bean, halved and
  seeds scraped (or for other
  flavourings, see Variation,
  below, or Panna Cotta
  Variations, page 144)
160 g egg yolk (about 8)
1 whole egg

To serve
caster sugar
nut pralines or candied nuts,
  crushed, for sprinkling
  (see page 196)

Preheat the oven to 110°C (Gas ½).

Place the cream, half of the sugar and the vanilla bean and seeds (or the flavourings of your choice) in a heavy-based saucepan and bring to the boil, stirring constantly.

Stir the remaining sugar into the egg yolk and whole egg. Drizzle in one-third of the hot cream mixture and stir to combine, then stir in the rest of the cream mixture. Strain through a sieve into a large jug.

This mixture is enough to fill ten 140 ml-capacity moulds, but you can use any size you like. Place your chosen moulds into a large baking tray lined with a tea towel or kitchen paper to stop them slipping around during cooking.

Divide the mixture among the moulds and pour boiling water into the tray to come three-quarters of the way up the moulds.

Cover the entire tray with foil and carefully place into the oven, taking care not to slosh the water into the moulds. Cook for 45 minutes (for 140 ml moulds) or until the creams have a wobble to them. They shouldn't be liquid still or cooked to soufflé stage either. Remove from the waterbath, then refrigerate until chilled.

TO SERVE
You can either brûlée the tops or simply scatter with the nut praline or candied nuts. To brûlée, evenly sprinkle the surface with sugar and use a kitchen blowtorch to caramelise the sugar. Repeat this process for each cream to create a beautiful crackable glaze.

VARIATION
• **Replace half of the sugar with honey and top with cashew and sesame praline.**

Bread 'n' Butter Pudding

I like to add medjool dates to this well-loved classic. They add sophistication and richness. It's a great way to use up left-over brioche too.

Serves 6–8

500 ml thickened cream
   (35% milk fat)
250 ml milk
1 vanilla bean, halved and
   seeds scraped
1 cinnamon stick
finely grated zest of 1 orange
5 egg yolks
1 whole egg
150 g caster sugar, plus extra
   for dusting
600 g brioche (see page 68)
   or good-quality white bread
butter, softened, for greasing
200 g medjool dates, pitted
   and torn into quarters

To serve
icing sugar, for dusting
pouring cream or vanilla
   ice-cream (see page 134)

Preheat the oven to 150°C (Gas 2).

Bring the cream and milk to the boil in a saucepan with the vanilla bean and seeds, cinnamon and orange zest.

Stir the egg yolks and whole egg in a heatproof bowl, then add the caster sugar. Add the hot cream mixture, a little at a time, whisking as you go.

In the meantime, break the brioche into rough golf ball-sized hunks. Butter a 2 litre-capacity baking dish generously with butter, then dust lightly with caster sugar. Arrange the brioche in the dish and disperse the dates between the layers.

Strain the cream mixture through a sieve over the brioche. Allow to soak for some time (about 1 hour), pushing the brioche pieces down occasionally as they soak up the liquid and become quite squishy.

Dust with caster sugar and bake for 50–60 minutes or until golden and set.

TO SERVE
Enjoy the pudding hot, dusted with icing sugar, with cream or ice-cream on the side.

VARIATION
*   **Replace the dates with raisins soaked in a fortified wine or rum.**

Fruit Tartlets

These morsels rely on simplicity, so use fruit at its peak: pears and quinces in winter; peaches and berries in summer; and figs and blackberries in autumn. Use whichever flavoured frangipane takes your fancy.

Makes 8

Tartlet shells
½ quantity (550 g) pâte sucrée
  (see page 44), chilled

Filling
1 quantity almond frangipane,
  pistachio frangipane or
  hazelnut frangipane or
  a variety (see page 104)
your choice of poached pears
  (see page 156), perfectly
  ripe peaches (peeled),
  or fresh blueberries,
  raspberries, strawberries,
  figs or blackberries
apricot or raspberry jam,
  for glazing

NOTE
- Some of my favourite
  combinations are peach
  and hazelnut frangipane,
  fresh blueberries and
  pistachio frangipane,
  and poached pear and
  almond frangipane.

FOR THE TARTLET SHELLS
Preheat the oven to 180°C (Gas 4). Line a baking tray with baking paper and place 8 cm-diameter by 1.5 cm-deep tart rings on top.

Follow the instructions on pages 38–41 to work the pâte sucrée with the heel of your hand until homogenous and supple but not soft. Roll into a log. If the pastry becomes too soft, put it back in the fridge to firm up a little.

Slice rounds off the log of pastry and roll out the slices to a thickness of 4 mm. Press the pastry into the tart rings, allowing the excess to overhang the rings. Refrigerate the tartlet shells for about 30 minutes to firm up the pastry.

Blind bake the tartlet shells (see page 42) for 15 minutes or until golden all over. Remove the foil and allow to cool slightly.

Using a small serrated knife, trim the overhanging pastry from the rim.

FOR THE FILLING
Pipe the frangipane into the tartlet shells, remembering to leave space for rising (see pages 106–7). Bake the frangipane as is and top with your choice of fresh fruit later, or if you would like to bake the fruit, add whichever fruit you are using (except strawberries). This should take 10–12 minutes for plain frangipane or 12–15 minutes with fruit. Test if they're cooked; the frangipane should spring back when pressed.

Meanwhile, warm the jam with a splash of water in a small saucepan until liquid, then pass through a sieve.

Remove the tarts from the oven and, while still hot, brush with the warm jam. Allow to cool before lifting off the rings and top with fresh fruit (if using).

Rice Pudding with Poached Dried Fruit

This childhood favourite is glammed up with the addition of dried fruit poached in fortified wine. It's perfect for a late-autumn dinner party or equally good with fresh strawberries and poached rhubarb in early spring.

Serves 8

Rice Pudding

1.1 litres milk

200 ml thickened cream (35% milk fat)

150 g caster sugar

1 vanilla bean, halved and seeds scraped

1 cinnamon stick

2 finger-length strips of orange zest (use a peeler and remove excess pith) (see Notes)

1 clove (see Notes)

220 g pudding, short-grain or carnaroli rice

3 gold-strength gelatine leaves (6 g), soaked in iced water until softened, then squeezed to remove excess water (see Note, page 142)

1 quantity (750 g) crème pâtissière (see page 132), at room temperature

250 g whipped cream (soft peak stage) (see page 122)

FOR THE RICE PUDDING

Place 8 individual dessert rings on a baking tray lined with baking paper.

Bring the milk, cream, sugar, vanilla bean and seeds, cinnamon, orange zest and clove to a simmer in a large heavy-based saucepan. Add the rice and cook over low heat, stirring occasionally, until the rice is tender. This takes up to 20 minutes, a little more for carnaroli rice. Add the gelatine and stir to dissolve.

Allow the pudding to cool, covered with plastic wrap. When cooled to blood temperature, remove all the aromatics.

Now stir through the crème pâtissière, then the whipped cream. Spoon into the rings (or divide among small serving bowls). Leave at room temperature until serving (or chill if serving with summery accompaniments). $\longrightarrow$

NOTES

- Don't forget to wash citrus fruits when using the zest.
- So the clove doesn't get lost, poke it through one of the strips of zest.

Life is uncertain.
Eat dessert first.

ERNESTINE ULMER

Poached Dried Fruit

200 g prunes
200 g dried apricots
100 g golden raisins (sultanas)
100 g dried baby figs
300 g caster sugar
375 ml fortified wine (such as
    Tokay, Muscat or Sauternes)
1 litre water
1 cinnamon stick
½ vanilla bean (or rinse the vanilla
    bean from the rice pudding)

To Serve

honey, for drizzling
sablé Breton (see page 52)
    or pâte sablée biscuits
    (see page 44), to serve

NOTE
• If you don't have access
  to a kitchen blowtorch,
  wipe the exterior of the
  ring with a tea towel
  dipped in very hot water,
  then unmould.

FOR THE POACHED DRIED FRUIT

If you have the time, poached dried fruit tastes better prepared several days ahead.

Soak the fruits separately in hot water for several hours or until plump and moist, then drain.

To make the poaching syrup, bring the remaining ingredients to the boil in a heavy-based saucepan. Reduce the heat to a simmer and add the drained fruit. Cover with a cartouche (see Note, page 160) and poach gently for about 1 hour or until swollen and soft. Allow the fruit to cool in the syrup.

Keep at room temperature, if using immediately, or store in the fridge. It will keep well for up to 1 week due to the high alcohol content but make sure it is completely submerged in the syrup.

TO SERVE

To unmould the rice puddings, place each on a serving plate and use a kitchen blowtorch to heat the outside of the ring, then gently lift off the ring (see Note). Surround and top each pudding with the poached dried fruit and drizzle with some poaching syrup and a little honey. Serve with a biscuit.

Alternatively, if presenting in a large serving bowl, top with the poached dried fruit, drizzle with the syrup and honey and let guests serve themselves.

Tiramisu

Italian for "pick me up", tiramisu is my favourite dessert featuring coffee. It lives up to its perky name with its winning combination of coffee and creamy mascarpone. Although considered a new "classic" dessert (only becoming popular in the 1980s), it's one I make time and time again. Here is my version, with a double hit of coffee flavour and spiked with very grown-up Italian liqueurs.

Serves 8

Zabaglione

120 g caster sugar

150 ml Marsala

6 egg yolks

500 g mascarpone

Syrup

150 ml very strong esspresso
  (about 3)

100 ml sugar syrup, at room
  temperature (see Note)

80 ml Marsala

50 ml Strega or Galliano liqueur

50 ml Amaretto liqueur

1 teaspoon liquid coffee extract
  (see Note, page 224) or instant
  coffee granules

FOR THE ZABAGLIONE

Whisk the sugar, marsala and egg yolks over a saucepan of barely simmering water until the mixture reaches 60°C — it should be pale and thick and feel warm to the touch.

Transfer the mixture to the bowl of an electric mixer fitted with a whisk attachment and continue whisking until cool and holding soft peaks.

Add the mascarpone and whisk on medium speed until combined. Take care that you don't over-whisk the mixture or it will split and appear curdled.

FOR THE SYRUP

Combine all of the ingredients in a bowl and stir well. ⟶⟶

NOTE

- **To make a simple sugar syrup, combine equal parts sugar and water and bring to the boil, stirring to dissolve the sugar. Allow to cool.**

To Assemble

1 quantity génoise (baked
   in a brownie tray) (see page 82)
100 g amaretti biscuits, crushed
   (optional)
200 g crème Chantilly
   (see page 124)
200 g best-quality dark
   couverture chocolate
   (see page 26)
cocoa powder, for coating

NOTE

- I use Trablit, which is
  a French liquid coffee
  extract. You can buy
  it from specialty food
  suppliers or online.

TO ASSEMBLE

You can make one large tiramisu (to fill a 2 litre-capacity serving dish) or 8 individual (250 ml-capacity) portions.

Cut the sponge cake widthways into 1.5 cm-thick strips. Load the zabaglione into a piping bag and pipe a 2 cm-thick layer in the base of your dish or glasses. Dip the cake strips one by one in the syrup and layer side by side over the zabaglione. Sprinkle on some of the amaretti, if you are using it. Continue layering until all the zabaglione and sponge cake strips are used up. Top with the crème Chantilly and spread evenly with a palette knife.

Break up the chocolate and pulverise in a food processor until it resembles fine gravel. Toss in a little cocoa powder, then scatter generously over the surface of the tiramisu. Refrigerate for at least 2 hours before serving.

Coffee makes
it possible to
get out of bed.
Chocolate makes it
worthwhile.

AUTHOR UNKNOWN

Summer Pudding

This is a wonderful dessert to showcase beautiful berries in season.
I like to mix in some frozen fruit too as they bleed lots of juice. I use plain panettone
for this pud as I think white bread can become a bit slimy. If you do want to use
white bread, make sure it is a very good pain de mie. Brioche works nicely too.

Serves 10 generously

1 loaf plain panettone
150 g fresh raspberries
150 g fresh blueberries
150 g fresh blackberries,
    loganberries or boysenberries
500 g frozen mixed berries
    or redcurrants (but not
    strawberries; see Notes)
200 g caster sugar

You will need to begin this recipe the day before (or 2 days ahead if you have the time).

Freeze the panettone for several hours before using (see Notes).

Carefully mix the fresh berries together and divide into two batches. Refrigerate half until serving.

Slice the semi-frozen panettne lengthways into 1.5 cm-thick slices and trim to fit into a 1 litre-capacity loaf tin (I like to use a 30 cm x 10 cm loaf tin), or a pudding basin, for a more traditional look if you prefer. Line the tin with a double layer of plastic wrap (see Notes), leaving ample overhang to wrap around the pudding.

Put the frozen berries, sugar and a splash of water in a heatproof bowl and put over a saucepan of barely simmering water. Cook, stirring occasionally, until the sugar has dissolved and the berries have given up their juice. Allow to cool. Gently fold through the remaining fresh berries.

⟶

NOTES
- Freezing the bread makes it easier to cut into very thin slices.
- Strawberries "cook" in the freezer, making them taste jammy. Fresh ones that have been cut for a few hours also develop an unpleasant flavour and texture.
- Dampen your tin with a little water or spray with cooking oil to help the plastic wrap adhere.

Seize the moment. Remember all those women on the Titanic who waved off the dessert cart.

ERMA BOMBECK

To Serve

pouring cream or crème anglaise
(see page 126)

TO ASSEMBLE

Put the lined tin on a large plate or tray to catch any overflow of juices. Line the tin with the panettone, trimming it to cover the base and sides. Spoon half of the berry mixture into the tin, then add a layer of panettone. Fill the tin with the remaining berry mixture, adding just enough of the juices to ensure the mixture in the tin is wet but not swimming with liquid. Remember, the panettone is very absorbent and the resulting pudding should be vibrant red.

Fold the excess plastic wrap around the pudding and poke a few holes in the top to allow excess liquid to drain out. Weight down the surface with a piece of cardboard, trimmed to fit, topped with a brick or some food tins. Refrigerate overnight or preferably for 2 days for the juices to soak in and the flavours to meld.

TO SERVE

Invert the pudding, still wrapped in its plastic wrap, onto a chopping board and cut into 3 cm-thick slices. Unwrap each slice and place on a serving plate. Garnish with the reserved fresh berries and serve with cream or crème anglaise.

Signatures

Peach Melba for Oprah

Poire Belle-Héllène

Snow White and Rose Red

Pain Perdu with Blood Plum and
Blackberry and Yoghurt Sorbet

Sablé Breton with Roasted Figs,
White Chocolate Mousse and Port

PS Snickers

Mille-feuille with Citrus Fruits and Basil

Raspberry and Chocolate Délice
with Brownie Ice-cream

Pineapple Doughnuts
with Gingerbread Ice-cream

Sauternes Crème Caramel,
Thyme-Roasted Apricots and
Almond Roly-Poly

Peach Melba for Oprah

I was very excited to be invited to create a dessert for Oprah when she visited our shores in November 2010. My inspiration was, naturally, Melbourne and I instantly thought of combining our beloved Peach Melba with macarons for their O-shape — my nod to Oprah's name. I love the pairing of peach and citrusy lemon verbena ice-cream, but if you have trouble finding the leaf, classic vanilla ice-cream is equally as good.

Serves 6

Macarons step 1

225 g pure icing sugar, sifted
225 g almond meal
85 g fresh eggwhite

Macarons step 2
— Italian meringue

225 g caster sugar
55 ml water
85 g dried eggwhite
(see Note)

NOTE
- **Leave the eggwhite for the second mixture at room temperature for several days to "dry out". This will ensure good inflation of the meringue.**

FOR THE MACARONS

Preheat the oven to 200°C (Gas 6). Line a large heavy-based baking tray with a silicone baking mat or baking paper.

STEP 1

Pulverise the icing sugar and almond meal in a food processor until very fine. Rub this mixture through a sieve. It is important that it is very fine and aerated, so if it's not fine enough, you may need to reblitz it after sieving. Whisk the fresh eggwhite briefly until foamy.

STEP 2 — ITALIAN MERINGUE

Meanwhile, put the sugar and water in a saucepan over medium heat and stir with your fingers until dissolved a little, then brush any crystals down from the side of the pan using a pastry brush dipped in cold water. Bring to the boil over medium heat and allow to bubble away undisturbed, without stirring or shaking the pan, until the syrup reaches 118°C.

Place the dried eggwhite in the bowl of an electric mixer and begin whisking on high speed.

When the sugar syrup reaches 121°C, remove the syrup from the heat and allow the bubbles to die down. At this stage the eggwhite should be holding soft peaks. Reduce the speed and carefully pour the hot syrup down the side of the bowl. Once all the syrup has been added, increase the speed and whisk until shiny and holding firm peaks (see page 102–3). ⟶

Poached peaches

6 poached peach halves
    (see page 161)
250 ml peach poaching syrup
    (see page 161)

To serve

450 g fresh raspberries
lemon verbena ice-cream,
    recently churned
    (see page 137)
edible gold leaf (see Note)

NOTE
- Edible gold leaf, usually
  22 or 24 carat, is available
  in gossamer-thin sheets
  from specialty baking stores
  or online. Use tweezers or
  fingers to handle the sheets.

STEP 3 — COMBINING

In a large bowl, make a paste with the almond meal mixture
and whisked eggwhite from step 1. Fold in one-third of the
Italian meringue from step 2, then fold in the remaining
meringue. Loosen the thick mixture by "beating down"— give
it several firm whacks with a wooden spoon to knock out some
of the air. The mixture should be sticky and flow off the spoon.

Put the mixture into a piping bag fitted with a 1.5 cm-plain
nozzle. Pipe 8 cm-diameter circles onto the baking mat or
prepared tray. You will need 12, but pipe more so you have
spares. Leave the macarons in a warm dry place for up to
1 hour, depending on the temperature, to form a "leathery"
skin which ensures a good "foot" or base.

Place in the oven and immediately turn off the heat. Leave
for 5 minutes, then turn the oven to 100°C and bake for
20 minutes. Remove from the oven and allow to cool
completely on the tray before gently removing.

FOR THE POACHED PEACHES

If refrigerated, drain the poached peaches on paper towel and
bring to room temperature.

Place the peach poaching syrup in a wide-based saucepan over
medium heat and cook until reduced by half to form a glaze.

TO SERVE

Using the tip of a small knife, very carefully remove the domed
tops off six of the macarons and discard (or eat) the tops
(you should have some spare just in case you break any).

Place the peach halves on top of the hollowed-out macarons.
Place a macaron onto each serving plate and arrange the
raspberries around the circumference. Pipe or spoon the
ice-cream into the cavity, then top with the peach macaron.
Lightly brush the peach with the glaze, decorate with a little
gold leaf and serve immediately.

I want a good body –
but not as much
as I want dessert.

JASON LOVE

Poire Belle-Héllène

My version of Escoffier's classic seems to be missing something at first? Where's the chocolate sauce? On the plate, it appears very simple, but crack the warm chocolate biscuit and honey-scented chocolate sauce flows out. Then dig into the pear and you'll discover it's filled with vanilla-flecked ice-cream. I love surprising people.

Serves 6

Poached pears

6 perfectly ripe pears
(William, Packham
or Bartlett)
625 g caster sugar
1.5 litres water
1 vanilla bean, split and
seeds scraped

Chocolate sauce

240 g best-quality dark
couverture chocolate
(see page 26)
155 ml milk
50 ml thickened cream
(35% milk fat)
30 g honey
50 g butter, cubed

FOR THE POACHED PEARS

Follow the instructions on page 156 to prepare the pears and poach them using the quantity of sugar and water given on the left. Add the vanilla bean and seeds to the pan when the sugar has dissolved. Allow the pears to cool in the syrup, then refrigerate until chilled.

FOR THE CHOCOLATE SAUCE

Finely chop or grate the chocolate and put in a bowl. Bring the milk and cream to the boil with the honey. Pour the hot cream mixture over the chocolate and stir until smooth and shiny. Add the butter, bit by bit, stirring until combined. Refrigerate the chocolate sauce until firmly set.

Now put the chocolate sauce into a piping bag fitted with a 1.5 cm plain-nozzle. Line a small tray with baking paper. Pipe the chocolate sauce into lines about 10 cm long.

Place in the freezer for about 30 minutes or until hard enough to cut into 5 cm lengths. Return to the freezer until needed.

$\longrightarrow$

NOTE
- You can make the poached pears, chocolate sauce and ice-cream ahead of time (but churn the ice-cream close to serving), but the biscuits need to be baked when you're ready to eat them.

Chocolate Biscuit

115 g best-quality dark
    couverture chocolate
    (at least 70% cocoa solids;
    see page 26)
50 g butter, cubed
40 g almond meal
40 g rice flour
80 g eggwhite
80 g caster sugar
40 g egg yolk (about 2)

FOR THE CHOCOLATE BISCUIT

Cut six strips of baking paper measuring 7 cm x 5 cm. Spray the inside of six 4.5 cm diameter dessert rings with cooking oil spray and line each with a strip of paper so that the paper forms a collar above the ring. Spray again and place on a baking tray lined with baking paper.

Finely chop or grate the chocolate and melt in a heatproof bowl over a saucepan of barely simmering water. Let more than half of the chocolate melt before you give it a stir with a wooden spoon or rubber spatula. When the chocolate has melted, turn off the heat and add the butter. Stir to combine and keep warm.

Sift together the almond meal and rice flour.

Whisk the eggwhite until holding soft peaks. Sprinkle in the sugar and whisk until shiny and holding firm peaks (see pages 102–3).

Place the egg yolk in a large bowl. Add one-quarter of the eggwhite mixture to the egg yolk and whisk to combine. Add this mixture to the chocolate mixture along with the dry ingredients. Thoroughly fold through, then fold in the remaining eggwhite mixture.

Place the mixture in a piping bag fitted with a 1.5 cm-plain nozzle. Pipe the mixture two-thirds of the way up the prepared rings.

Remove the 5 cm lengths of chocolate sauce from the freezer and insert one into each chocolate cylinder, taking care not to touch the base. Pipe in more mixture to fill each cylinder. Freeze for at least 3 hours.

Remove the cylinders from the freezer 1 hour before serving, but keep in the fridge.

Preheat the oven to 180°C (Gas 4). Place the cylinders in the middle of the oven and bake for 12 minutes. Remove from the oven and leave for a couple of minutes before unmoulding.

To serve
vanilla ice-cream
(see page 134), recently
churned (see Note)

NOTE
• Try to churn the ice-cream
close to serving otherwise
it will be too difficult to
pipe. If it is too firm, place
it in the fridge to soften
a little.

TO SERVE

Drain the pears on paper towel and discard the poaching syrup.

Gently slip a palette knife underneath each chocolate biscuit and lift off the rings. Remove the paper collar and place each biscuit on a serving plate.

To finish, fill a large piping bag fitted with a small plain nozzle with the ice-cream and pipe the ice-cream into the cavity of each pear. Place next to the biscuits and serve immediately.

Snow White and Rose Red

Inspired by the fairytale of the same name, this is the ultimate "girly" dessert. As this dessert is primarily ice-cream and sorbet, it's best kept for small gatherings, otherwise making scoops of ice-cream and sorbet to serve more than four guests could prove a challenge and a puddle of mess.

Serves 4

Baked Rhubarb

1 quantity disgorged rhubarb
  (see page 162)
375 ml Moscato or
  sparkling wine

Angel Wings

1 quantity French meringue
  mixture (see page 100)

FOR THE BAKED RHUBARB

Preheat the oven to 150°C (Gas 2).

Tip the entire contents of the disgorged rhubarb into a baking dish that will fit the rhubarb snugly in one layer and pour over the wine. Cover with foil and bake for 20 minutes or until the rhubarb is tender. Cool in the syrup. You can make this 1 day ahead and store in the syrup in an airtight container in the fridge.

FOR THE ANGEL WINGS

Preheat the oven to 90°C (Gas ¼). Line a baking tray with baking paper.

Put the meringue in a piping bag fitted with a 1 cm-plain nozzle. Pipe 3 cm blobs onto the prepared tray. Using the back of a teaspoon, in one sweep, smear the blobs to resemble wings. You will need 8 wings. This quantity will make more than enough but it's good to have spares because they break easily.

Bake for 1 hour, then remove from the oven and cool on the tray completely before gently peeling off the paper. You can make these up to 1 day ahead and store in an airtight container until needed.

⟶

There is
nothing wrong
with me
a little ice cream
won't fix.

AUTHOR UNKNOWN

Strawberry juice
500 g perfectly ripe
strawberries
50 g caster sugar

To serve
250 g perfectly ripe
strawberries
strawberry sorbet
(see page 168)
rose geranium ice-cream,
recently churned
(see page 137)
12 crystallised red or
white rose petals (or a
combination of both is
preferable) (see page 200)

FOR THE STRAWBERRY JUICE

Follow the instructions on page 106 to make the strawberry juice, using the quantities given at left.

TO SERVE

Using a small melon (parisian) scoop, make strawberry balls from half of the strawberries. Slice the remaining strawberries into rounds.

Drain the baked rhubarb and divide among dessert glasses. Place a scoop of strawberry sorbet in each glass, then a scoop of rose geranium ice-cream. Scatter over the strawberry balls and slices, then top with another scoop of sorbet. Drizzle with some strawberry juice, decorate with the angel wings and rose petals and serve immediately.

NOTE
- It's easy to prepare most of the components ahead of time and assemble just before serving. Bake the rhubarb and make the sorbet and angel wings the day before. Make the ice-cream base the day before, too, and churn just before serving.

Pain Perdu with Blood Plum and Blackberry and Yoghurt Sorbet

I love the combination of warm fruit, sticky brioche and cold sorbet in this dessert. The polka-dotted sorbet is one of my favourites to make because it looks so pretty on the plate. The colours of the fruits all come together for a knockout presentation.

Serves 4

Pain Perdu

1 large double loaf of brioche
 (see page 68)
250 g caster sugar
200 ml water

FOR THE PAIN PERDU

Preheat the oven to 180°C (Gas 4) and line a baking tray with baking paper.

Cut the brioche into 3.5 cm-thick slices, then into 9 cm x 3 cm blocks. Discard the scraps (see Note).

Bring the sugar and water to the boil, stirring until the sugar has dissolved, then cool.

Dip the brioche blocks into the cooled sugar syrup and roll around to soak well. Drain on paper towel.

Heat a large non-stick frying pan over medium heat. Add the brioche and cook until golden brown on all four sides. Take care as they will burn quickly. Once nicely coloured, put on the prepared tray. Put in the oven and reduce the temperature to 120°C (Gas ½) to warm through. ⟶

NOTE
* Any left-over brioche can be saved to make Bread 'n' Butter Pudding (see page 214).

Sablé Breton with Roasted Figs, White Chocolate Mousse and Port

This is a stunning visual feast to finish a dinner party. During summer,
I like to substitute fresh berries for figs or even balls of different coloured melons.

Serves 8

Tart shell
1 quantity sablé Breton
(see page 52), at room
temperature
plain flour, for dusting

Port syrup
375 ml vintage port
200 g caster sugar
finely grated zest of 1 orange
1 vanilla bean, halved and
seeds scraped

NOTE
- **Allowing the port syrup
to cool ensures that the
aromatics infuse well.
Also, once cool, any foam
or bubbles will not pass
through the sieve.**

FOR THE TART SHELL

Preheat the oven to 165°C (Gas 2–3). Spray a 22 cm-diameter
by 4 cm-high dessert ring with cooking oil spray and
lightly dust with flour. Place on a baking tray lined with
baking paper.

Lightly dust a work surface with flour and gently press the
sablé Breton into a disc. Roll out to 2 cm-thick and large
enough to fit the dessert ring. Slide the pastry onto the ring
and press it up the sides slightly to form a border (see page 57).

Bake for 20–25 minutes or until puffed up and golden brown.
Allow to cool in the ring. The pastry will sink down slightly
as it cools.

FOR THE PORT SYRUP

In the meantime, make the port syrup. Combine the port,
sugar, orange zest and vanilla bean and seeds in a small
heavy-based saucepan and bring to a simmer over medium
heat. Continue cooking until the syrup has reduced by half.
Allow to cool completely (see Note), then strain through
a sieve, discarding the aromatics.

$\longrightarrow$

There is nothing better than a good friend – except a good friend with chocolate.

LINDA GRAYSON

Roasted figs
7–8 perfectly ripe figs
(green or black or a
combination of both)
caster sugar, for dusting

To assemble
1 quantity white chocolate
mousse, chilled
(see page 148)
white chocolate curls
(see page 190)

FOR THE ROASTED FIGS

Increase the oven temperature to 190°C (Gas 5). Line a baking tray with foil.

Halve the figs and place, cut side up, onto the prepared tray. Dust generously with the sugar. Bake for 10–12 minutes or until soft but not falling apart. While still warm, brush the roasted figs with some of the cooled port syrup (reserve left-over port syrup to serve).

TO ASSEMBLE

To unmould the tart shell, place on a serving plate and run a small knife around the edge, then gently lift off the dessert ring.

Now begin "building" the dessert by alternating quenelles (see page 140) of mousse with the roasted figs. When the whole surface of the tart is covered, build up in the centre so the dessert has a domed top rather than looking flat like a pizza. Drizzle with the remaining port syrup and decorate with the chocolate curls.

NOTE
- You can assemble the tart up to 3 hours ahead before drizzling over the syrup and adding the chocolate curls.

PS Snickers

My decadent and extremely rich tribute to the Snickers bar. It's all about the salted peanuts. The method is quite involved but the result is well worth the effort and you can make all of the components ahead and just assemble right before serving.

Serves 12 generously

Caramel parfait
   Step 1 — Caramel
300 ml thickened cream
   (35% milk fat)
115 g liquid glucose
1 vanilla bean, halved
   and seeds scraped
140 g caster sugar
50 g butter, cubed
3 gold-strength gelatine
   leaves (6 g), soaked
   in iced water to soften,
   then squeezed to remove
   excess water (see page 142)

Caramel parfait
   Step 2 — Bombe
50 g caster sugar
20 g liquid glucose
60 ml water
160 g egg yolk (about 8)

Caramel parfait
   Step 3 — Combining
200 g whipped cream (soft
   peak stage) (see page 122)

FOR THE CARAMEL PARFAIT

Line a 30 cm x 20 cm brownie tin with baking paper (with the corners cut out so it sits flush).

STEP 1 — CARAMEL

Put the cream, liquid glucose and vanilla bean and seeds in a saucepan and bring to the boil.

Meanwhile, heat a heavy-based saucepan over medium heat until 1 teaspoon of the sugar melts when sprinkled in. Gradually add the remaining sugar and stir constantly until all the sugar has melted and is light golden brown. Be careful not to let the caramel become too dark or it will taste bitter.

Slowly pour the hot cream mixture onto the caramel, whisking until combined. Whisk in the butter, then the gelatine. Strain into a metal bowl and set aside to cool, whisking occasionally.

STEP 2 — BOMBE

Put the sugar, glucose and water into a small saucepan and bring to the boil, stirring with your fingers to dissolve the sugar slightly, then brush any crystals from the side of the pan with a pastry brushed dipped in water. Continue to cook, without stirring, until the syrup reaches 118°C.

Meanwhile, place the egg yolk in the bowl of an electric mixer fitted with a whisk attachment and beat on medium speed to lightly break up.

Once the sugar has reached 118°C, remove from the heat and let the bubbles die down slightly. Reduce the speed of the electric mixer to medium and, while whisking, pour the syrup down the side of the bowl onto the egg yolk. Increase the speed and whisk until the mixture has cooled. ⟶⟫

Milk chocolate mousse

250 g best-quality couverture
   milk chocolate (see page 26)
150 ml base crème anglaise
   (see page 126)
225 g whipped cream (soft
   peak stage (see page 122)

Salted peanut caramel

200 ml thickened cream
   (35% milk fat)
120 g caster sugar
80 g liquid glucose
50 g butter, cubed
100 g salted peanuts, roughly
   chopped

To assemble

1 quantity dacquoise
   (see page 96)
24 milk chocolate plaques
   (8 cm x 4cm) (have some
   spares just in case;
   see page 194)

NOTE

- You can make the chocolate plaques well in advance. The caramel parfait will keep in the freezer for 3–4 days, well wrapped. The chocolate mousse and salted peanut caramel will hold up well refrigerated for several days, but the dacquoise should be made on the day of serving.

STEP 3 — COMBINING

Remove the bowl from the mixer and gently fold the bombe from step 2 and the cooled caramel from step 1 together, then fold in the whipped cream. Pour the parfait into the prepared tin and freeze for several hours until firm.

FOR THE MILK CHOCOLATE MOUSSE

Follow the instructions to make the mousse on page 148, using the quantities given at left. Refrigerate to set.

FOR THE SALTED PEANUT CARAMEL

Follow the method to make the caramel on page 253. Fold through the peanuts and keep at room temperature until needed.

TO ASSEMBLE

Remove the caramel parfait from the freezer and allow to sit at room temperature for 10 minutes or until the surface becomes slightly sticky.

Place a piece of baking paper on the surface of the dacquoise and carefully flip it over. Remove the paper. Now invert the parfait onto the dacquoise and press down lightly so that the two surfaces stick together nicely. If the parfait is getting too soft, return it to the freezer for a while. Using a large knife heated under very hot water, cut the parfait–dacquoise slab into 8 cm x 4 cm logs, taking care to keep the edges clean and straight. Return to the freezer until ready to serve.

TO SERVE

Put a small blob of the chocolate mousse in the middle of each serving plate. This will stop the Snickers from sliding around. Then place each log, dacquoise side down, on a plate. Now peel the plastic off a chocolate plaque and carefully place, shiny side up, on top. Using a teaspoon dipped into very hot water, form small quenelles (see page 140) of chocolate mousse and place three evenly on each Snickers. Fill the gaps between the mousse with the salted peanut caramel, then place another plaque on top (don't forget to peel off the acetate). Serve immediately.

Don't wreck a sublime chocolate experience by feeling guilty.

LORA BRODY

Mille-feuille with Citrus Fruits and Basil

I love the combination of citrus and basil. This dessert has everything:
the tang of the fruit, the sweet crunch of the puff pastry and the unctuous
pale green basil cream. It's my sophisticated version of a French classic.

Serves 6

1 quantity puff pastry
   (see page 58), chilled
60 g pure icing sugar

Citrus fruits
1 ruby grapefruit
2 oranges
2 blood oranges
2 mandarins
1 tangelo

Preheat the oven to 190°C (Gas 5). Line a heavy-based baking
tray with baking paper.

Lightly dust a work surface with flour. Using firm, even
strokes, bash the pastry out to a workable thickness with a
rolling pin, then roll out to about 4 mm thick. Using a pastry
docker or a fork, prick the pastry all over (see Notes). Place
onto the prepared tray. Cover the surface with another layer
of paper and place two heavy trays on top. If you don't have
a third tray, weight the top down with something heavy.

Bake for 15-18 minutes or until golden. Remove from the oven
and take off the top trays and the paper. Increase the oven
temperature to 220°C (Gas 7). Using a sieve, heavily dust or
dredge the pastry with the icing sugar.

Return the pastry to the oven and bake until the sugar
caramelises, about 4-6 minutes. Don't turn your back on it,
as the pastry can burn quickly. Remove from the oven and
allow to cool, then cut into 10 cm x 4 cm rectangles.
You will need 18 rectangles.

CITRUS FRUITS

Peel and segment the citrus fruits using a very sharp knife
(see page 178). Cut the grapefruit segments in half. Try and
do this as close as possible to serving as the juices will leach
out if prepared too far in advance.

$\longrightarrow$

NOTES
- Docking or pricking the
  pastry will help keep the
  layers from puffing up
  too much during baking.
- You can use any
  combination of citrus
  fruits that are in season.

Vegetables are
the food of the earth;
fruit seems more
the food of the
heavens.

SEPAL FELICIVANT

Basil cream
1 cup basil leaves
finely grated zest of
   1 orange
80 g caster sugar
375 ml thickened cream
   (35% milk fat)
150 ml milk
2 gold-strength gelatine
   leaves (4 g), softened
   in cold water, then
   squeezed to remove
   excess water
   (see page 142)

To serve
confit orange zest strips
   and pearls (see page 180)
tiny basil leaves,
   for garnishing

FOR THE BASIL CREAM

Blanch the basil leaves in rapidly boiling water, drain then refresh in iced water. Drain again and squeeze out the excess water. Roughly chop.

Rub the orange zest into the sugar to release the citrus oils (see page 176). Put the cream and milk in a saucepan, add the orange zest mixture and bring to a simmer, stirring to dissolve the sugar. When the liquids come to a simmer, add the gelatine and stir to dissolve.

In a blender, whiz the basil and half of the cream mixture until completely puréed and vivid green. Add the remaining cream mixture. Strain through a fine sieve into a container and refrigerate until set.

TO SERVE

Place a little confit zest on the serving plates (this will stop the pastry from slipping), then place a pastry rectangle on top. Using a teaspoon dipped into very hot water, form small quenelles (see page 140) of the basil cream and place evenly onto the pastry. Fill the gaps in between with the citrus fruits. Scatter confit orange zest strips between them. Place another pastry rectangle on top and repeat. Top with a final layer of pastry, and garnish with confit zest pearls and the tiny basil leaves.

NOTE
- The puff pastry dough can be made ahead and frozen but it is best baked on the day of serving or the sugar becomes sticky. You can make the confit zest well ahead and the basil cream the day before, but segment the citrus fruit just before serving.

Raspberry and Chocolate Délice with Brownie Ice-cream

This elegant dessert never fails to induce swoons and with good reason. The brownie is all grown up in this elegant dessert, and it's a great way to use up brownie crumbs so they don't go to waste.

Serves 6

Ganache

275 g best-quality couverture milk chocolate

100 g best-quality couverture dark chocolate (see page 26)

80 ml thickened cream (35% milk fat)

110 g caster sugar

110 g raspberry purée

70 g butter, cubed

To assemble

1 quantity chocolate sponge cake, at room temperature (see page 94)

450 g perfectly ripe fresh raspberries

6 dark chocolate plaques (8 cm x 8 cm) (have some spares just in case; see page 194)

1 cup crumbled brownie (see page 114)

vanilla ice-cream, recently churned (see page 134)

FOR THE GANACHE

Line a 25 cm x 15 cm brownie tin with baking paper.

Roughly chop the chocolates and put into a food processor. Meanwhile, bring the cream and sugar to the boil in one saucepan and the raspberry purée in another pan. Turn on the food processor and pour in both the hot liquids. Continue to process until smooth and shiny.

Add the butter and blend until it is all incorporated. Pour the ganache into the prepared tin and chill until firm (several hours or preferably overnight).

TO ASSEMBLE

Chill six serving plates. Flip the ganache onto the slab of sponge cake. Remove the baking paper from the ganache and, using a knife dipped in very hot water, cut the slab into 6 cm squares. Place onto the chilled plates and surround each square with the raspberries. Carefully top each with a chocolate plaque.

Sprinkle a layer of brownie crumbs over the surface of the ice-cream and, using a large dessertspoon dipped into very hot water, roll up the ice-cream around the crumbs. Place the scoop in the centre of the chocolate plaque. Repeat for each plate. Serve immediately.

Pineapple Doughnuts with Gingerbread Ice-Cream

This is my play on the old corner-store classic. The spicy candy aromas of the syrup and the luxurious gingerbread ice-cream elevate the humble doughnut to new heights.

Serves 6–8

Spiced syrup

1 perfectly ripe pineapple

50 g butter

2 tablespoons chopped
   fresh ginger

1 vanilla bean, halved
   and seeds scraped

1 cinnamon stick

100 g caster sugar

50 ml passionfruit juice
   (pulp from 3 passionfruits
   pushed through a sieve)

To serve

1 quantity freshly made hot
   doughnuts (see page 108)

tiny mint leaves,
   for garnishing

3 passionfruits, halved

1 quantity gingerbread
   ice-cream, recently churned
   (see page 138)

FOR THE SPICED SYRUP

Using a very sharp knife, peel the pineapple and remove the "eyes". Cut lengthways into 8 pieces, remove the core and set the core aside to infuse the syrup. Cut or break the pineapple pieces into bite-sized chunks and reserve for serving.

Melt the butter in a saucepan over medium heat. Add the ginger, vanilla bean and seeds, cinnamon and sugar and stir over medium heat until the sugar dissolves.

Finely chop the pineapple core and add to the pan along with the passionfruit juice. Simmer until reduced by half. Remove from the heat and set aside to infuse for 30 minutes. Strain through a sieve, discarding the solids. Set the syrup aside at room temperature.

TO SERVE

While the doughnuts are still hot, roll in the spiced syrup along with the reserved pineapple chunks.

Arrange the doughnuts and pineapple chunks on serving plates. Spoon over a little of the spiced syrup, scatter over the mint leaves and spoon over the passionfruit pulp. Using a small spoon dipped into very hot water, form a quenelle (see page 140) of ice-cream and place on each plate. Serve immediately.

Sauternes Crème Caramel, Thyme-Roasted Apricots and Almond Roly-Poly

This sexy dessert showcases many different textures and cooking methods.
My version involves a lot of separate components but it is well worth the effort.
All the elements (except the apricots) are best prepared the day before.

Serves 8

Almond roly-poly

150 g apricot jam

1 tablespoon Amaretto
(optional)

1 quantity freshly made
biscuit joconde, at room
temperature (see page 88)

Caramel

200 g caster sugar

100 ml cold water

40 ml hot water

NOTES
- When making the caramel, this stage is crucial. If the caramel is too light, it will dissolve too much and be insipid. But if it is too dark, it will taste bitter.
- I prefer to use metal dariole moulds rather than plastic ones as they conduct heat better, making them easier to unmould for serving.

FOR THE ALMOND ROLY-POLY

Place the cake on a piece of baking paper and trim the edges.

Warm the apricot jam with a splash of water in a small saucepan over medium heat until liquid, then pass through a sieve. Add the amaretto (if using) to the jam and set aside to cool.

Using a pastry brush, paint a generous layer of the jam over the surface of the sponge. Lift the corners of the baking paper to help roll the cake into a log **lengthways.** Wrap the log tightly in plastic wrap and refrigerate until needed.

FOR THE CARAMEL

Put the sugar and water into a small saucepan and bring to the boil, stirring with your fingers to dissolve the sugar slightly, then brush any crystals from the side of the pan with a pastry brushed dipped in water. Allow to bubble away, untouched, until it starts to colour. Swirl the pan at this stage and continue to cook until golden and it has just started to slightly smoke (see Notes). Now add the hot water, taking care as it will splutter. Swirl the pan to combine the water until the bubbles have died down.

Divide the caramel among eight 125 ml-capacity dariole moulds (see Notes). Set aside while you prepare the crème caramel base.

$\longrightarrow$

Crème caramel base

finely grated zest of 1 orange
90 g caster sugar
375 ml Sauternes or good-
  quality sweet wine
645 ml thickened cream
  (35% fat)
4 gold-strength gelatine
  leaves (8 g), softened in
  iced water, then squeezed
  to remove excess water
  (see page 142)

Almond praline

200 g blanched almonds,
  carefully split in half
200 g caster sugar
40 ml water

Thyme-roasted apricots

12 perfectly ripe apricots
3 sprigs thyme
caster sugar, for sprinkling
butter, for dabbing

To serve

edible gold leaf (see Note,
  page 234) (optional)
crystallised yellow rose petals
  (see page 200) (optional)

FOR THE CRÈME CARAMEL BASE

Rub the orange zest into the sugar (see page 176) and combine with the wine in a saucepan. Bring to a simmer, then add the cream. Stir until the mixture comes back to a simmer, then add the gelatine and stir to dissolve. Pour into the moulds and refrigerate for at least 4 hours but preferably overnight.

FOR THE ALMOND PRALINE

Follow the instructions on page 196 to make the praline, using the quantity of almonds and sugar given at left, but leave the almonds as halves. When you pour the hot nuts onto a tray, use two forks to separate the halves while they're still warm. Leave to cool and set, then store in an airtight container until needed.

THYME-ROASTED APRICOTS

Preheat the oven to 190°C (Gas 5). Line a baking tray with baking paper.

Split the apricots in half and place cut side up onto the prepared tray. Sprinkle the cut surface generously with the sugar and scatter over the thyme sprigs. Dot each with a little of the butter and roast until heated through and fragrant. This will take about 10 minutes and is best done just before serving.

TO SERVE

Dip the dariole moulds into very hot water to loosen the crème caramels and to dissolve the caramel, then turn out onto serving plates. Cut the roly-poly into 24 slices and arrange on the plates. Add three roasted apricot halves to each plate and dot with gold leaf (if using). Scatter over a few praline almonds and crystallised rose petals (if using).

Dessert is probably the most important stage of the meal, since it will be the last thing your guests remember before they pass out all over the table.

WILLIAM POWELL

Index

Index

Index

Metric Conversions

WEIGHT

Metric	Imperial
10–15 g	$^1/_2$ oz
20 g	$^3/_4$ oz
30 g	1 oz
40 g	$1^1/_2$ oz
50–60 g	2 oz
75 g	$2^1/_2$ oz
80 g	3 oz
100 g	$3^1/_2$ oz
125 g	4 oz
150 g	5 oz
175 g	6 oz
200 g	7 oz
225 g	8 oz
250 g	9 oz
275 g	10 oz
300 g	$10^1/_2$ oz
350 g	12 oz
400 g	14 oz
450 g	1 lb
500 g	1 lb 2 oz
600 g	1 lb 5 oz
650 g	1 lb 7 oz
750 g	1 lb 10 oz
900 g	2 lb
1 kg	2 lb 3 oz

TEMPERATURE

°C	°F
140	275
150	300
160	320
170	340
180	350
190	375
200	400
210	410
220	430

VOLUME

Metric	Imperial
50–60 ml	2 fl oz
75 ml	$2^1/_2$ fl oz
100 ml	$3^1/_2$ fl oz
120 ml	4 fl oz
150 ml	5 fl oz
170 ml	6 fl oz
200 ml	7 fl oz
225 ml	8 fl oz
250 ml	$8^1/_2$ fl oz
300 ml	10 fl oz
400 ml	13 fl oz
500 ml	17 fl oz
600 ml	20 fl oz
750 ml	25 fl oz
1 litre	34 fl oz

LENGTH

Metric	Imperial
5 mm	$^1/_4$ in
1 cm	$^1/_2$ in
2 cm	$^3/_4$ in
2.5 cm	1 in
5 cm	2 in
7.5 cm	3 in
10 cm	4 in
15 cm	6 in
20 cm	8 in
30 cm	12 in

TEASPOONS, TABLESPOONS & CUPS

1 teaspoon = 5 ml
1 tablespoon = 20 ml
1 cup = 250 ml

Acknowledgements

I'd like to thank the inspiring team involved in the creation of this book. From Hardie Grant, Gordana Trifunovic for her no-nonsense yet highly enthusiastic approach to getting this book published; Belinda So for being so patient and enormously helpful editing my scribbles into clear and useable recipes; Leesa O'Reilly for her amazing styling, sourcing the gorgeous props and for being lovely to have around during the photo shoot; Mark Roper and his assistant Peter for the stunning photography and for taking most of the leftovers off my hands; Gayna Murphy for the great combination of glamour, practicality and realness to the design; and Paul McNally for convincing me to convince him that this would make a beautiful and useful addition to anyone's recipe book collection.

Thanks to Ally from Simon Johnson for the chocolate. Big thanks to my talented sister Josephine for her keen eye for design and being my stunt hands when necessary! I would also like to thank my talented assistant Keum Hwa Lee for her attention to detail and for doing all the "fiddly bits" so beautifully.

Having prepared and photographed all these pictures at home, I must thank my patient partner Andrew for helping me wipe chocolate off the walls and sugar from the floor. And thanks to Donovan, my darling son, for all the invaluable advice and for helping with the taste-testing.

And, above all, thanks to my wonderful ma Bet for a lifetime of inspiration and encouragement!